Understanding Arthur Miller's

- A complete GCSE Study Guide for iGCSE English Literature students for 2016 exams

By Gavin Smithers

Another one of **Gavin's Guides** - study books packed with insight. They aim to help you raise your grade!

Understanding Arthur Miller's All My Sons is a complete study guide and has been written for both students and teachers who are preparing for GCSE in 2016 and beyond.

Series Editor: Gill Chilton

Published by Gavin's Guides

The complete text of "All My Sons" is widely available, and is published by Penguin Books. You will need a copy of the text of the play to use alongside this study guide.

**822
MIL**

Let's get started

"All My Sons" was the first real success of the American playwright Arthur Miller's career as a dramatist. It is one of four of his plays which frequently feature as set texts for English Literature exams. The others are "The Crucible", "Death of a Salesman" and "A View from the Bridge". Watching or reading any of them will help to inform your study of the others, because Miller's preoccupations remain the same.

Miller examines the conscience of a hero, or a family group, or a small community; he creates a difficult situation or a crisis, and tests their integrity and their morals. Miller is interested in whether we do the right thing under extreme pressure. His sympathy lies with the victim, the character who is overwhelmed and engulfed by the brutal, stifling pressure to conform. He cannot conform, because his is a type of behaviour which has already made him stray or lose his way. This is either anti-social, or heroic, depending on your point of view; or, for an audience, it is both!

This guide is designed for students who will sit the Cambridge IGCSE English Literature specification 0486 in June 2016. **You will have 45 minutes to write an essay, based on either a passage or an extract printed in the question paper, or on the play as a whole.** Depending on your school or college, your exam may be either open text or closed, when you will not be able to take a copy of the play into your exam with you. It will be worth 25% of your English Literature GCSE.

Your exam is designed to provide a fair test; to give you the opportunity to show that you know the play and its plot, that you understand the role and function of each character, that you have an engaged response of your own to Miller's meaning and message, and that you can explain how Miller uses language in his drama. This guide will help you with all of that!

Gavin's Guides work because of their attention to detail, and the space that each guide devotes to showing how the author manages and organises our response as we read.

It is understanding this – and being able to communicate that you do to your examiner - that will mean you can achieve a good grade more easily.

Several of Miller's plays present the central character as an ordinary, or "little" man, who makes a serious error of judgment- either an illicit love affair, or a moral crime of some other kind- tries to keep it a secret, and is forced to face the consequences when the truth finally comes to light.

While these errors of judgment, and the subsequent cover-ups, deserve to be condemned (hypocritically, by the society Miller's heroes live within, and less so, by his audience in the theatre), we feel pity and empathy for these heroes, who acquire a tragic status through the courage with which they finally face the loss of their place in society, and their right to continue living.

Miller himself had an adulterous affair with the actress Marilyn Monroe; he was married three times; he was susceptible to the seductive power of the illicit. He was also a determined advocate of intellectual freedom in America, and critical of many of the values of American society, especially its tendency to be narrow-minded, intolerant and exaggeratedly individualistic. We can often detect the herd or mob mentality in the background of these plays.

We are used to soap operas and dramas where the action flows in real time. By contrast, here Miller uses dramatic tension in an interesting and powerful way, **by having the key event, secret or betrayal happen long before the play starts**. In "All My Sons", we do not even know what the secret is, until more than half way through the play- we just know that an associate of Joe Keller's is in prison, and that he himself had been first convicted and then acquitted of a crime.

The fact that it involved manslaughter (as a result of shipping faulty engine parts) is held back; as is the key link with Larry's death, which proves- much, much later- to be a suicide, motivated by Larry's shame at what his own father had done.

The inversion of the natural order- parents should die before their children, not the other way round- mirrors the clever and dramatic reversal of the plotting process; the characters and the audience know *less* than Joe, the tragic hero (who hides his secret shame); *normally, in the genre of tragedy, the audience knows more*. It can usually see the consequences- the car crash which is about to happen- before the tragic hero can.

In "All My Sons", Miller makes the climax of the play short- Act 3 is very short- and quite brutal.

He makes his tragic characters disintegrate much more quickly than Shakespeare does, with Othello or Macbeth. This technique of shortening the approach to the summit of the play heightens our sense of shock, and it makes us more empathetic towards the "little man" who is both the architect and the victim of his own tragedy.

I am a private tutor in Broadway, Worcestershire, and this book was initially written for my English Literature students. I wrote it to help them achieve good grades – and an understanding of what this original, succinct writer wanted to say. Now in paperback, I hope it may help you too.

"All My Sons" in context

Arthur Miller is one of the most distinguished playwrights of the twentieth century. He was born in New York City in 1915, and died in 2005, aged 89. His father owned a factory which manufactured clothing; he employed 400 people. The business failed during the Wall

Street Crash of 1929. Arthur Miller married Mary Grace Slattery in 1940, and was excused from serving in the Army because of an injury. His first play was produced in 1944, but, although it had won a critical award, it was a commercial disaster.

"All My Sons", by contrast, was a success when it appeared in 1947. Miller's next play, "Death of a Salesman", built on some of the themes of "All My Sons", in 1949. It has become one of the most acclaimed of all modern plays. Miller followed that with "The Crucible" in 1953; another celebrated play, which is a commentary on American politics, individual conscience and freedom of speech.

He went on to write more than twenty plays, and he explained his methods and interests in an important "Introduction to the Collected Plays" in 1958. He explains that he wants to make his plays "realistic" by characterising, in some depth, what the people in them want to achieve; their motivations must make them interesting and convincing as individuals.

He is conscious that any human being has some principle which they will not back down from, and which leads to the crisis in a play. Joe's is the absolute priority of passing his business to his surviving son; Chris's priority is to live a "better" life because of the sense of social responsibility the war has given him; and so on. Miller sees the potential for tragedy in that personal choice, which we can describe as obsessive and anti-social- it leads people to choose not to conform to what society expects of them, even if they must die as a consequence.

Miller explains that, in his first professionally staged play, "The Man Who Had All the Luck", he wanted to explore "what exact part a man played in his own fate". He then became preoccupied with father-son relationships, and when he heard the story that a man had been taken to the police by his own daughter for selling defective machinery to the Army, he found he now had all the elements of "All My Sons".

The drama would hinge on a decision which leads his own family to ostracise a father- "the revelation of the full loathesomeness of an anti-social action".

He describes Joe Keller as "a threat to society" because Joe refuses to see himself as personally responsible; he hides behind the defence that other people were profiting from the war in the same way as him. This way of looking at your world is something, Miller believes, we need to be protected from, unless the world is to become a jungle, a space without any collective identity, where sheer size and ferocity hold sway.

"All My Sons" is a tragedy. Joe Keller shoots himself at the end of Act 3, because he believes that this is now the only way of atoning for his moral crime of supplying fatally dangerous engine parts for military aircraft. He can no longer pretend that he was not responsible for his own son's suicide, because his wife Kate cannot pretend any longer either.

Miller was interested in tragedy as a dramatic genre, and in its principles, which come from the traditions of the theatre in ancient Greece. He wanted to take the tragic model (defined by Aristotle in his "Poetics") and make it modern, and relevant to his own times.

Greek tragedy was adapted and developed by Shakespeare (and other dramatists) - Othello, Macbeth and King Lear fit the genre well. The theory of tragedy (established by Aristotle) states that the tragic hero must die at the end of the play, because he (and it is usually a man) has a flaw in his character and has made a fatal mistake, so bad that it means he forfeits his place in society. The key quality, in Greek tragedy, is "hubris"- a form of pride or arrogance which leads the tragic hero to break the rules of personal and social morality, because he thinks- arrogantly- that they do not apply to him.

The tragic hero deserves to die, because of the severity of his mistake; but the audience must feel fear and pity- fear that, if we were in their position, we might well have done the same, and pity, because we feel the crushing magnitude of the punishment - death, not just as a price to pay, but as a symbol of exclusion from civilised society.

Joe Keller is an accidental murderer (Keller is an off-key spelling version of "killer"). His sin is ignoring the fact that the faulty engine parts are extremely dangerous: he persuades himself that somehow it doesn't matter, that somehow things will turn out well. He faces the prospect of losing the business he has devoted forty years of his life to, if he admits to an unreliable production process and loses his contract with the army. His behaviour is cowardly and morally wrong, but there are mitigating circumstances. Joe is a hard-working man, devoted to his family because, instead of growing up in a secure home, he was, himself, put out to work at the age of ten. He has little education, and not much intelligence; Miller compares him with a peasant, and tells us that, for Joe, making decisions is hard. He is often uncertain in the play, and he constantly seeks advice or direction from his wife and his surviving son.

Because what Joe does is the result of who he is, the audience feels sorry for him, while we are also critical of his lack of bravery and principles in making his key decision - which goes back three and a half years. That decision leads directly to the deaths of twenty-one pilots and to the suicide of his own son. ✸

His determination to keep his crimes a secret (with the help of his wife, Kate) has led to the imprisonment of his former business partner, Steve Deever. It obstructs (and perhaps ruins) his older son's hopes of a happy family of his own with Ann Deever, and it has made Kate nervous and clinically ill - she has continual chronic headaches and insomnia, and her sanity seems to be genuinely fragile.

Joe had been criminalised too, but he took his case to an appeal, and managed to pin all the blame for the faulty cylinder heads on Steve.

He went on to recover his own reputation, and he expanded his factory business, so that his own comfort has been built on the ruins of the devastation he has condemned the Deever family to. This is doubly devious, selfish and cowardly.

The play shows us the truth emerging, so that the consequences of it become impossible to ignore any longer; Miller called this an "unveiling". Classical tragedy hinges on the idea that the outside world- the cosmos- somehow has a self-correcting mechanism; individuals' misdeeds emerge and are punished, so that the world is put right again, because the rules of proper behaviour have been reasserted, by eliminating those who deviate from the rules of the society they live in.

More modern dramatists are more subtle about how their tragedies end. In Shakespeare, the world will miss Othello's energy but not his naivete. The ending of "King Lear" does not hold out the prospect of a gentler world, whereas in "Hamlet" something – normality- is restored.

For Miller, the range and scope of the tragedy is rooted securely within the family, and less within a civic world. It is Joe's lack of conscience which makes him, in Chris' terms, less than human, and disqualifies him from living. The wider community will not be conscious of Joe's departure from the world (barring, perhaps, a news story in the local paper), but the surviving members of his family- Kate and Chris - will no longer have to labour under the weight of the lies which have been choking the Keller family with years of watchful, strained self-deception.

Joe Keller has very little about him which is innately noble or admirable; really, just his attachment to his family. In classical tragedy, the hero is usually a man with a leadership role - a king, or general - and a string of successes and achievements, often patriotic. Miller prefers to make his heroes less heroic- almost anti-heroes - and to make his tragedies more domestic, because the dilemma a tragic hero faces is the same, whether he is a Greek king or an "ordinary Joe".

Miller's individual variant of the tragic genre shows us that there is something potentially heroic about the struggle of the "little man"- an uneducated, unskilled citizen, born without advantages or privileges - and his destruction by the world he lives in - small-town (or big city) America.

Here, Miller is similar to his fellow American, the novelist John Steinbeck ("Of Mice and Men", "The Grapes of Wrath"), but Steinbeck writes with more pathos - he presents his protagonists more thoroughly as victims, who can never win their battle to survive and pursue legitimate personal dreams. Joe Keller dies, too, but only after he has enjoyed apparent (financial) success, though it is built out of lies and blood, so that his downfall is deserved, but also sad for the audience to witness.

⭐ Joe Keller's personal needs are modest, and he shares his tobacco and his newspaper with anyone who wants them. As we shall see in the commentary section, Miller is so successful at making us empathise with Joe - despite his limitations - that we tend to forget, for most of the play, just how serious his error is. Perhaps this is why Miller gave him the "Keller" surname- to avoid any doubt that he is a virtual killer, of twenty-one young pilots, and of his own son. ✦

In the best known of all Greek tragedies, Sophocles' "Oedipus Rex", Oedipus kills his father and marries his mother (unaware of who she is). Miller has a father killing a son instead; and he has Kate pronouncing that "God does not let a son be killed by his father". This is the law of the universe which Joe cannot be allowed to break; but he has broken it already.

 A note on themes

The play raises questions about our *moral responsibility* - to *our family* and to *society* in its wider sense. It is, in some ways, an American equivalent to the English author, JB Priestley's "An Inspector Calls"; it presents us with parents who want to preserve their status and position in society, even though they have a scandal to keep secret, and adult children who reject this approach and demand that, as people, we must, in future, all be "better" than we have been i.e. more virtuous in our behaviour.

Joe and Kate both use *avoidance* as a way of dealing with the past - by not facing it. They can avoid Joe's guilt because the court has absolved him, because there is no proof that Larry is dead, and by pretending that Steve deserves to be in prison. The dramatic tension in the play comes from the remorseless way in which the plot removes each of these pillars of avoidance, so that the hollow structure of Joe's and Kate's life comes crashing down around them.

Miller said that he wanted to address an issue which people felt intuitively, but did not acknowledge - that, because so many Americans were individualistic and greedy, they had profited personally from the Second World War in an improper way. This was an exceptionally bold statement to make, coming as it did just two years after the war had ended.

Chris' discomfort, and his struggle to settle into post-war society, reflects the guilt or shame of the survivor. Miller's intention is that, after the end of the play, Chris will continue to run the business, but he will do so ethically.

It would be wrong to see the play as a criticism of *the American dream.* The play does not define capitalism or entrepreneurship as being wrong. Joe's situation, as the owner of a manufacturing business, gives him the potential to make a disastrous choice. That he chooses the wrong option is not because he is a capitalist - it is because he is an American, and poorly educated. The self-interest which underpins his crime - his belief that all that matters is his own family - comes from the prevailing values of the society he lives in, and which has produced him. It is only Chris' experience of a different world, in the war, and his sense of responsibility, which enables the audience to judge, as Chris does, that Joe's world is a "zoo"- a place inhabited by caged animals, who should be living life "better".

Commentary & Analysis

Now we go on to the close reading of the text itself.

We might think that the play would be easier to analyse if it were divided into separate scenes, or into Acts of roughly the same length. Act 1 is 46% of the play; Act 2 is 39%. This seems off-balance, but Miller needs to write the play in long, continuous Acts in order to reveal, or "unveil", the truth, in small snippets, through the dialogue.

At the heart of Miller's dramatic technique, there lies a neat device. The play itself is about the damage done when people (like Joe, Ann, George, Kate) shrink from confronting the truth, or dealing with awkward situations. Look at the "mini-scenes", when a character leaves the stage or avoids a conflict, and you will find Miller inserting another short scene, which postpones or avoids the action which really needs to take place.

Minor characters such as Frank and Bert usually appear at moments of high tension, and put off its resolution. This is a little like real life; but, for the dramatist, it is also a way of preserving and building dramatic tension. Miller keeps us on the edge of our seats, waiting for Ann, waiting for Larry, waiting for George, waiting for the truth…….. and then he delivers the truth, like the descent of the blade of a guillotine, with Larry's letter.

The lengths of Acts 1 and 2 are therefore a structural feature of the play, dictated by the shape of the plot, which reveals, slowly but inexorably, a long-hidden truth about events from three years ago or more. Miller needs the time and space to explain not just who has hidden what, but what sort of people they are and what sort of lives they want, or say they want. Without the complicating empathy we feel for Joe and Kate, the play would not be a tragedy. It would simply be a crude morality play, like some tale of murder and retribution from the Wild West.

Act 1

The play is set in August, at the back of the Kellers' house, which is in the suburbs of an unspecified town. It is private or "secluded" because it is screened with trees. The other tree in the yard is the shattered apple tree, which is broken into two pieces; the symbolic meaning of this apple tree remains to be spoken of. The scene is domestic, private, and peaceful, on an "early Sunday morning"; the mood of relaxation will be broken, in Act 2, when George arrives.

Act 1 takes up almost half of the length of the play. It provides most of the necessary background to the dramatic climax at the end of the (very short) Act 3.

Joe is sharing his newspaper with Jim Bayliss, who asks him to share his tobacco too. Joe is very willing to, and, a little later, he shares the parsley they have grown, with Sue. Frank arrives; they discuss what is in the paper - only bad news, according to Frank, who asks, innocently, "What's today's calamity?". Today's calamity will soon be the exposing of the Kellers' lies, and the suicide of Joe.

Joe is interested in how people make a living - a sign of how important to him the notion of respectability by occupation is - and he says that occupations and professions are not as clear as they used to be, "in my day". He says that reading the papers reminds him of "how ignorant" he is; how little he knows, himself - how little he understands the wider world. To some extent, he chooses to live in ignorance, because, for him, that is easier than living with the truth.

Frank mentions that the shattered apple tree, broken in last night's storm, is Larry's tree. It is clear that Larry is dead - Joe refers to that as a fact. But, oddly, Frank is preparing Larry's horoscope, at Kate's request, to see whether November 25th, the day on which he was "reported missing", was his "favourable day"; if it was, then, according to Frank, he may still be alive. This is irrational and pure superstition. Jim, a doctor of medicine, says that Frank, in believing this, is "completely out of his mind"; so, in fact, is Kate, though she is ill with grief and the constant stress of maintaining the edifice of lies about her husband's innocence.

Frank criticises Jim ("you don't *believe* in anything") while Jim critics Frank ("you believe in *anything*"). This talk about what you believe in is important, because it serves to show that even a slight change of emphasis - as with this phrase, which the two men conflict with - can be symptomatic of a big difference in attitude. As the play unfolds, everything Chris has *believed* about his father's integrity and honesty is destroyed; George and Ann have to start *believing* in their own father's innocence; Kate will have to give up her half-imagined, *irrational belief* that Larry is still alive. No-one will still be able to believe that Joe was not responsible for the deaths of Larry and the other pilots.

In the play, truth, knowledge and belief are associated closely. What characters know "in their heart" is often an unacknowledged truth, which they do not believe in fully, for fear of the damage it could do to their relationships with others.

Jim's young son wants to be a doctor. Jim expresses his own frustration with his career. He "would love to help humanity" by doing medical research, but it is badly paid, so his wife will not let him. This revelation hints at the compromises and lack of fulfilment which the men in this play feel, because they have a duty to make money to support their wives and families; Kate Keller and Sue Bayliss insist upon it.

The Baylisses and the Kellers are neighbours in a suburb of a small American town, and they share the same outlook - that the only call our society has on us is the call to fight in a war. Apart from that, they believe that the prosperity of their own family is all that matters. Their *thinking* (not just their way of life) lacks any awareness that they live in a community or society wider than this. This is why Joe pays no regard to the possible implications of shipping the defective engine parts, beyond what shipping them or not shipping them means for his family and his family business.

This early snippet of conversation, about the stars, and about men being unable to do the work they want to, prepares for an important scene where Jim talks to Kate, at the beginning of Act 3.

The first scene or episode – the conversation between Joe, Jim and Frank - ends when Jim asks about "the beautiful girl". This is Ann, who had arrived on the train at one o'clock that morning, and is asleep upstairs. Jim would like to be able to see "a pretty girl", and we understand why, when his wife Sue appears, calls him a dog, and encourages him to visit Mr Hubbard (who is not ill) for a fee.

Sue is about forty (like her husband), and overweight- Miller uses her size as a physical sign of her greed for money and consumption. The Baylisses speak to each other disrespectfully; familiarity breeds contempt and frustration. Their rather cynical and bitter exchange includes a rude joke about Jim telling his patient Mrs Adams to lie down. Jim has allowed his wife to brow-beat him into being untrue to himself; Kate has influenced Joe in the same way, although, as she tells him, his desire to please at home is no excuse for what he did.

Joe says that their previous neighbours, before Jim and Sue, were "a very happy family"; he does not name them, but it was the Deevers. Why these happy neighbours left is not mentioned; the hint is that the Baylisses are not so happy, while, of course, the apparently calm and happy life of the Keller family is about to come to a sudden and violent end.

Jim Bayliss is bossed around and told what to do by his unattractive wife; that is why a "beautiful" or "pretty" girl would have a powerful influence on him, as a welcome distraction.

Joe tells Sue that she is "too…..realistic". He seems to mean "materialistic", but either does not know the word or does not dare offend her by using it. The word "realistic" almost sounds like a compliment, instead.

If, by "realistic", Joe means shrewd, or adaptable to the price people will pay for the attention of a doctor (even when they are not ill), then we inevitably ask ourselves how far the term applies to him, too. His defence of his refusal to do the difficult, but right, thing over the faulty engine parts is that there was no realistic or practical alternative, because he would have lost his business. That is realistic, but deeply wrong.

Sue leaves the stage, making way for Lydia. She and Frank are married (to each other) and they are light, largely comic characters. She cannot make the toaster work, and the explanation is that she has not plugged it in! In the middle of this short scene, Lydia asks Joe whether Ann is still in mourning for Larry. Joe expects her to be ready to move on, and marry ("it's a couple of years already"- this becomes three and a half years in Act 3); then Chris appears. The revelation that Ann's visit is taking place so that she can accept Chris' marriage proposal is deferred for several minutes in the play, until the boy Bert has appeared and left, and Chris and Joe are deep in a private conversation about the ongoing consequences of their habit of condoning Kate's wish to believe that Larry is still alive. Here, we see Joe avoiding conflict by not telling Kate the truth; it helps to define his character as an appeaser and a coward, rather than a teller of the truth.

Miller introduces Chris with a stage direction telling us that he is "a listener", and he is slow to say much. He reads the books section of the paper, and, like Joe, he is aware of his own "ignorance". They have nothing to say to each other about books. Neither of them reads any books and their lack of interest in education contributes to their lack of understanding.

Joe is concerned about Kate's reaction to the storm breaking Larry's tree; Chris is indifferent to it. But, before they can discuss their handling of Kate, there is a scene with Bert, in which the child and Joe play with the language of police investigation (inspection, policeman, detective, the jail, bars, gun, arrest). This is make-believe; its significance is only clear much later. The talk of jail jars with Kate; for Joe, it must be soothing to turn his fear of re-arrest and imprisonment into a game. The audience knows nothing yet of his previous, real-life arrest and imprisonment.

It is only with hindsight - when Joe talks about his release and homecoming - that we see how he has no scruples about reinventing the truth, to suit his own reputation. He did precisely this, in pinning the blame for his own decision and actions on his business partner.

Another apparently insignificant line is Joe's remark, about Tommy playing with a thermometer, that "there's no harm in (an) oral (reading)". Meaning attaches to this remark later, when we discover that Joe had promised Steve in their phone call that he would take responsibility for the decision to ship the faulty parts, but that, at his appeal, he denied that the conversation ever took place (George, in Act 2- "In a court you can always deny a phone call and that's exactly what he did"). This is the basis for Joe's acquittal - the "fast one" people say he "pulled" to be freed.

By contrast, the fact that Larry wrote his feelings in a suicide note means that his evidence cannot be ignored, as oral evidence can be.

The interlude with Bert ends with Chris joking that all the local children, in the guise of policemen, will come "and beat your brains out"; ironically, Joe's brains will be spilt, but only by himself, because he will shoot himself.

Chris and Joe now have a long conversation which reveals a good deal about the Keller family. They discuss the nocturnal wanderings, sleeplessness and grief of a woman they refer to as "she" and "her", before Chris identifies her as "Mother". He and Joe have worked together to conceal the truth from her, that Larry is dead (just as Joe had conspired with Steve Deever over the truth about the defective parts). Chris now calls the deception of his mother "dishonest....a terrible mistake".

Apart from Kate, "nobody believes Larry is alive", and Chris argues that they should not "allow her to go on thinking that we believe with her". We have already noted the importance of the word "belief", when Jim and Frank spoke about it.

Chris says that Kate even "dreams" that Larry is returning - she describes that dream when she appears - and that is her version of the American dream, which gives her "hope" (and so, by definition, it cannot be achieved- for American writers, time and again, the notion of the "dream" is a useful mechanism for engineering a character's failure to achieve it).

Joe is "frightened at the thought" of confronting her with the truth, because, with "no body and … no grave" she will never be persuaded. He knows that Kate is susceptible to feeling, not to logic (which points to Larry being dead, three years after being reported missing in combat); and he reminds Chris that the newspapers - which he is so reluctant to read - report the return of missing soldiers regularly. Later, we will find out that the lack of hard evidence (in writing) enabled Joe to win his appeal against his prison sentence. It is only Larry's letter which finally proves that he is dead. Only written evidence cannot be lied into obscurity.

Joe's fear comes from a deep-seated wish to avoid conflict. Chris, having been involved in terrible fighting in the war, has no such fear. Moreover, his motive is that he wants to marry Ann. In order for that to happen, Kate will have to concede that Larry is dead, so that there is no longer any reason for Ann to wait for him. Chris' desire for a family of his own is the first element in the plot which disturbs the smooth life of the Kellers, and requires them to acknowledge what is true and what is lies.

Joe and Chris are unable to agree on what to say to Kate - Joe wants to say nothing. Significantly, Chris presents the problem as one "we" need to deal with, but Joe throws the responsibility for solving it back on to Chris - he speaks of "you", not "us". His instinct here, his preference to avoid a tricky issue by choosing not to resolve it, is precisely how he behaved over the engine parts. Chris has warned him that lies always have a pay-off; we would say that they come back to haunt you. But Joe still does not see the need to disturb Kate or "argue with her".

Joe has a deeper fear, too; not just that Kate may harm herself (as she puts it, "if he's not coming back, then I'll kill myself") but that her world, and their family, will fall apart under the pressure of the truth, because, as Kate puts it to Chris, "if he's dead, your father killed him". Proof of Larry's death (his letter) is proof that Joe is guilty of the mass murder of twenty-one pilots, plus Larry- "all my sons".

Chris insists on telling Joe "why I asked Annie here". Although he has not seen her for five years, he says that "when I think of someone for my wife, I think of Annie". His dream is "beautiful. I want a family, I want some kids, I want to build something......Annie is in the middle of that".

He tells Joe that the family business "doesn't inspire me"; if he cannot make his dream come true here, he will move away, to New York or elsewhere. When he ends the conversation by saying "I'm a pretty tough guy", he means that he will not compromise on his plan to marry Ann.

Again, Joe tries to evade responsibility, arguing that Chris can marry whomever he likes, but that he must be careful to avoid upsetting his mother. Chris tells Joe that, in this habit of avoiding conflict at all costs, "you infuriate me.....you have such a talent for ignoring things".

Joe justifies his inaction by explaining "I ignore what I gotta ignore"- by which, he means, obliquely, the truth about his own behaviour, guilt and cowardice.

Chris complains that "every time I reach out for something I want, I have to pull back because other people will suffer". He thinks that marrying Ann will resolve this fundamental unhappiness, and the sense he expresses, that men always have to compromise, and give up their dreams, allies him with Jim, whom Sue did not allow to pursue the lower-paid career he really wanted.

Chris may be wrong to think that marriage brings men complete happiness. Certainly it doesn't bring full happiness to any of the married couples in this play. Examples of married couples not being happy include Joe and Kate, who disagree over how he has made his money, in their final private conversation in Act 3; Jim and Sue, who disagree about what is important; and Frank, married to an attractive girl, with children, who has no real drive or purpose.

The curse of the Keller family is that none of them can maintain their dream. Theirs has been built on depriving other families of the dreams they had, of their sons returning from the war; and on depriving the Deevers of their home, next door, and of their reputation.

Kate appears on stage for the first time, and she remains there for almost the whole of the remainder of Act 1. Miller's stage direction tells us that she is emotionally volatile ("uncontrolled").

There is some domestic trivia to begin with, but Joe refers to his past thoughts about "when I got money again"- Miller has him hinting at a financial misfortune, but he still keeps the details from us.

We hear that the Kellers have a maid, but they seem not to have adjusted to their affluence comfortably. Joe still puts the rubbish out; when he says "I don't like garbage in the house", there is hidden irony. If we regard lies as a form of rubbish, the Kellers have garbage everywhere!

Kate expresses relief that the storm has broken Larry's tree; a little further on, we understand why. She thinks that it is too early to have a memorial to him, because she believes he is still alive. Her superstition is out of control; she takes the conjunction of Ann's visit in the month of his birthday (she is sleeping in Larry's bedroom), her own tripping over his baseball glove, and the tree being damaged, as signs he is about to return. He is; but only in the shape of his letter, telling the truth about his own despair, shame and suicide; confirming that he is dead, and destroying Kate's self-delusion, along with Joe's.

She complains about the "funny pain on the top of my head", which is a recurring theme, and a sign of the emotional strain she is under. She says "It's not like a headache"; it is deeper and more serious than that.

Kate tells Chris that she does not know why Ann is visiting, but this public denial is designed just to deter Chris from raising the uncomfortable need to move on. As soon as she is alone with Joe, Kate goes straight to the question of her prohibiting the marriage. To Chris, she praises Ann for her loyalty to Larry and her apparent celibacy. Chris points out that the fact that Ann has not married does not mean she is waiting for Larry, or paralysed with grief for him.

Kate retaliates with the vivid account of her surreal dream of Larry flying overhead, and falling from his plane. She has been counting the number of times Chris has suggested that they should stop being so preoccupied with Larry ("That's the third time you've said that this week"). Chris talks, like a therapist, about the family's need to "break out of" the cycle of denial, but he cannot know yet that his mother is also in a form of denial about Joe's guilt, which Joe himself finds it easier to "ignore".

Perhaps Kate uses her headache here as a means of deflecting Chris from the confrontation which would follow if he announced that he were marrying Ann. That confrontation does take place, but not until the final scene of Act 2.

As soon as she is alone with Joe, Kate speaks more directly, without any hint of weakness or any desire to placate. Joe lies to her, to keep the peace, saying "he didn't tell me any more than he told you"- Chris has, in fact, told him directly that he is going to marry Ann, even if he has to move away from the area as a result.

Kate demands that Joe must "believe", as she does, that the storm and Ann's return are portents that Larry is coming back. Belief without supporting evidence is what we call faith. Kate's language here is full of the terminology of religion - faithful as a rock, her faith, he's coming back, believe with me, don't stop believing. For the believing Kate, the return of Larry is like the second coming of Christ - a redemptive, heavenly, and much longed for transfiguration.

Her threat to kill herself "if he's not coming back", and her physical shaking, offer some justification for Joe's passivity here - he does not have the same intense feeling, or her need for belief. Kate is adamant that Chris will not marry Ann ("I won't stand for any nonsense"; "He's not going to marry her"). Joe simply asks her, "What do you want me to do?"- just as he had asked Chris "What can I do for you?". He is at a loss whenever he is asked for emotional support, instead of money.

A second brief appearance by Bert links with the previous one, very early in Act 1. In a scene where just 69 words are said, we have the word **arrest**, and the word **jail** no fewer than four times - two of which also feature Joe's other interest, so that the phrase becomes "**jail business**". Kate is shaking, because the very word conjures up terrors (like Lady Macbeth's sleepwalking, and her vision of the murder she arranged). Joe asks, rhetorically, and with irony, "What have I got to hide?". It is only a few pages further on, when Joe talks about his release from prison on appeal, that we can see the reasons for Kate's hypersensitivity.

Just as Kate's motivations and behaviour had been discussed in some detail before she appeared on stage, Ann now makes a belated appearance; everyone has been waiting for her to emerge from the house. Miller's stage direction tells us that she is "gentle" but uncompromising - the other side of the loyalty or faithfulness which Kate so admires in her. Ann is publicly admired, for her clothes (Kate), her prettiness (Chris), her legs (Joe), and her apparent intelligence (Jim). Jim warns her not to "count your husband's money" (as Sue has always done) - he means she should not measure the success of her own future marriage in terms of financial wealth. Jim mentions that he fought alongside Chris ("in the Battalion").

Kate has an uncomfortable exchange with Ann, because she jumps "triumphantly" on any indication that Ann still "thinks of" Larry; her emotional extremism is at odds with Ann's realism, which can distinguish between the present and what is over- "those dear dead days beyond recall". Kate, like Jay Gatsby in F Scott Fitzgerald's "The Great Gatsby", clings to a dream which should be allowed to die - the dream, or illusion, that you can relive the past. Ann stares at Kate when she realises that the clothes and carefully shining shoes in the wardrobe are Larry's, not Chris' because maintaining this shrine to Larry is macabre and ghoulish, and a sign that she cannot and will not let go.

Kate is vulnerable, so that, when Ann describes her belief that Larry will return as "ridiculous", she retreats into her emotional bunker. She argues that survivors do come back, and that women like her are "still waiting for their sons…..in the dark at night", in a vigil, not for the dead, but for the living. She says that what we know has nothing to do with facts, but is about pure intuition, which we tap into by listening to our heart.

Her swivel-eyed insistence that Ann has "always been waiting" for Larry "deep, deep in your heart" is off-putting because it is extreme; Kate tells Ann that those who think otherwise - including Ann herself!- "don't know", so that she must not "let them tell you what to think". Kate tries to manipulate others into accepting her truth about the world, which is a surreal combination of her own fantasy and the superstitious, rather than what others can see, rationally, in the real world.

Ann is delicate and gentle, but also firm, in trying to ease Kate out of her obsessive belief that she, too, is simply waiting for Larry. But she has rejected her own father because of his apparent criminality; she does not care whether her parents' marriage survives his prison sentence, and she does not agree with Kate that Steve is "a decent man". Ann, like her brother George, has judged that the criminal is outside society, and excluded from his own family; it becomes clear, in Act 2, that neither of Steve's children has written to him or visited him. Chris will reject Joe in the same way, and it may be that the prospect of a long prison sentence with no contact from Chris makes suicide the preferable option for Joe at the end of the play.

Ann asks Kate to explain why she is so sure Larry is alive. Kate claims to have psychic powers about both her sons; ironically, she had needed no written evidence (a letter or a newspaper report) to know when Chris was in extreme danger in "that terrible battle". She claims that "there's God", and the existence of God is necessary, "otherwise anything could happen".

Kate believes in cosmic forces, because she finds that a convincing support for her own emotional needs- "certain things have to be, and certain things can never be". With hindsight, later in the play, we see a link between this remark of Kate's and her statement, near the end of Act 2, that "God does not let a son be killed by his father". To Kate, that is the unspeakable crime.

Ann disagrees with Kate, because she has Larry's letter; she knows that Kate's desperate attempt to construct a world in which fathers do not kill sons is contradicted by the written evidence; what we know in our heart, or think we do, cannot stand up against that. Kate argues that, because the sun rises every day, there is order in the world; without this comforting routine, "anything could happen". Ironically, the arrivals of Ann (at Chris' invitation), then George, disrupt the daily order of the Kellers' lives, and make real the "certain things" which "can never happen". Kate is mistaken, if she really believes that there is a God in Nature who will protect her and Joe; rather, there is a social order - of personal responsibility and morality - which is about to force their misdeeds into the open, and force Joe to make his peace with the world.

Ann contradicts Kate's view with the simplest of words- "No"- but the tension is defused, and an argument pre-empted, by the appearance of Frank, who is carrying a ladder. Joe tells Ann that Frank is going bald because "he's got responsibility". Frank is "still haberdashering"-

presumably, he supplies material and Lydia makes clothes- but he does not have a large factory like Joe's. Frank has something, though, which Joe does not - an honest and relaxed relationship with his wife and children.

His appearance in this short scene heads off the possible conflict between Ann and Kate. The dialogue also informs us that Ann's brother George has a degree - one of the reasons Joe fears him - and that Ann's father, whom Frank says is "intelligent", is in prison. Frank need not mention the reason; it is already well known to the characters, but Miller gains extra tension by keeping the audience ignorant of the story.

Frank admires Ann, and leaves, promising Kate that he will "finish the horoscope tonight". As it turns out, his superstitious finding - that Larry's plane went missing on his "favourable day"- is shown to be worthless when Ann reveals the letter and its explanation of why Larry has died, on that day, of all days- because of his intense sense of shame at what his father had done.

Ann feels the same shame, but - for now - about her own, criminally convicted, father. The dialogue shows us that Joe, on being released from prison himself, had "confused" the local children, who think that his "jail situation" is that he is a detective, not an excused criminal. Joe has rehabilitated his social standing by deceiving children as well as the adults in the neighbourhood. Ann remembers a mob shouting "Murderers" at both men. Joe tells her that, because all of those people come and play cards with him for money - and perhaps he is careful to lose to them? – the old accusations of guilt are forgotten now. Kate points out that they may have been put to rest because no-one wants to confront Joe, with his acquittal, but that they do, in fact, still regard Ann's father as a murderer.

Kate pretends that she was reluctant for Ann to visit because of what she might hear about her father. This is untrue; she wishes Ann had stayed away so that she could not threaten to marry Chris, and force the fact of Larry's death to be accepted.

Joe relates his version of his return home from prison. It sounds like a well-polished and rehearsed account. People thought he had "pulled a fast one"- lied, or bribed his way to an acquittal. People thought he was the Devil ("the beast"), and now Joe relates the crime- causing twenty-one planes to crash in Australia. Joe sees the "court paper in my pocket" as proof that he was not guilty, and could no longer be called a murderer. That enabled him to become "a respected man again", with a business "bigger than ever" fourteen months on.

Joe attributes courage to himself, in returning to face his critics and accusers, talk, smile and play cards with them. But his actions were really designed - as with his role as the detective in the children's games - to hide the truth. He tells Ann that her father should move back here, too, when he is released. Ann is dumbfounded that Joe should "forgive" a man whom she (wrongly) believes caused his unjust imprisonment; Joe says there is no point "crucifying" him.

Note two things here; first, the religious language, and secondly, how damaging it is when the truth is hidden. Who was crucified? Christ, the innocent Son of God; or, in Miller's play, Steve Deever, the innocent, naïve, "little" man who allowed Joe to make him responsible for something he was not to blame for.

Joe has no reason at all to resent Steve, knowing, as he does, that he is a scapegoat. Ann, who thinks that her father is guilty, as charged and convicted, "stares....mystified" at Joe's willingness to be his neighbour and associate again. The idea of loving your neighbour comes from the Old Testament in the Bible (Leviticus, Chapter 19), and it is worth reminding ourselves of other instructions which are recorded in the Old Testament too as being given to Moses by God - they prohibit dealing falsely, stealing and lying; bearing grudges; cheating commercially, by using false measures; cursing your own parents; taking (marrying) your brother's wife.

This is interesting, because Joe speaks, disapprovingly, of Chris' honesty and scruples in business ("you make a deal, overcharge two cents, and his hair falls out"); the play is set on a Sunday, which is the Kellers' maid's day off.

We find the Ten Commandments in the Old Testament, too (Exodus, chapter 20). They specify that your servants shall not work on Sundays, which are days of rest; "thou shalt not kill", "steal", or "bear false witness" against your neighbour; or covet his house, or anything which belongs to him; or commit adultery.

The Kellers allow their maid to have Sundays off, but, in other respects, they seem to be serial breakers of the religious or social laws of the Old Testament. This is a sign that they do not conform to, or feel any allegiance to, social norms which are to do with morality.

Miller's argument is both that Joe Keller is personally guilty of a terrible crime, and that Joe is the product of a society where the wholehearted approval of material success means that the compromises and wrong-doing which make that success possible also tend to be condoned, or ignored, by the society of which he is a citizen.

Reading the play, we have a sense that this is indeed a family and a community which pays lip service to the rules of society- there is no work on Sunday, and, although there is some cultural lust directed by married men towards attractive unmarried girls, there is no adultery. However, the Baylisses wanted the Deevers' house, and they occupy it; Chris plans to "take Larry's girl" (by proposing marriage to her); Joe, according to George, has stolen everything the Deever family had, and he has (accidentally) killed twenty-one young pilots, and, effectively, his own son; he has exploited the occasional client in his business career; and he has lied about Steve, and betrayed him.

Miller has created an ethos of social and moral values - of sin and righteousness - vaguely consistent with a more primitive or literal form of religion. He sets this as the opposite of Kate's desperate superstition, **but we sense,**

already, that wrongs must be put right, because the wheels of justice continue to turn, slowly, in some hidden part of the cosmos.

Ann reveals that she and her brother have rejected all contact with their father. They have ostracised him - put him out of the civilised community - because of the magnitude of his crime. Ann's judgment is unambiguous - although Steve is her father, the possibility that he is responsible for Larry's death means it would be "wrong to pity" him. This judgment - by the younger generation - is straightforward and objective. It rejects - in advance - Joe's argument that what he did was not wrong, because he did it for his family. Kate, too, will reject that defence unambiguously, in Act 3.

The hard line Ann and George have taken with their father (who is innocent) foreshadows the equally firm condemnation Joe will face from Chris in Act 3.

The children in this play have not yet been exposed to dilemmas in their own lives which demand difficult decisions, but their moral seriousness suggests that they would do the right thing - Joe, and Kate, have failed to do that. Kate insists that Ann must not mention the unmentionable - who is responsible for Larry's death - and she cuts Joe off when there is a small risk that he may say something which incriminates himself. In saying "He's not dead, so there's no argument", Kate avoids conflict, by ignoring the truth and maintaining the myth. She is still maintaining the myth at the moment in Act 3 when Ann finally resorts to Larry's letter as the proof that he is not alive.

Joe will not be silenced, however; he wants to explain to Ann that there is no connection between Larry and the faulty engine parts, because "Larry never flew a P-40". He then gives a speech which is just like a witness statement in a court of law. He represents Steve Deever as "a little man......always scared of loud voices", and he states that Steve was intimidated and pressurised by the heat and the demands of the Army into bodging a repair, and shipping the parts- "that's bad, that's wrong, but that's what a little man does". The implication is that he, Joe, would have done things differently.

Just as Kate clings to the lie she has created about Larry's survival, Joe has created his own false version of the critical moment, and he is a convincing liar, if he has not actually come to believe his own, revised, or reinvented, version of the truth.

He says that he would have stopped the faulty parts from leaving the factory "If I could have gone in that day"; and that shipping them was "a mistake, but it ain't murder". Once we find out, in Act 2, that Joe's absence that day was through cowardice, not illness, we can see that he is really seeking to defend himself, and his own actions, not Steve's. While Ann thinks he is being generous to Steve, he is in fact trying to let himself off the hook, because facing his own guilt would bring – and indeed it will bring - the carefully constructed "house of Keller" down with a crash.

Joe tells Ann "You mustn't feel that way". Joe cannot handle other people's emotionalism effectively - especially not Chris'

. There is a deep irony in the words he uses to finish his speech- "it ain't right". He is referring to Ann's judgment of her own father. It is, indeed, wrong because he – Steve - is innocent. But, at this point, the audience is as unaware of that as Ann is. She - and we - discover the truth in the middle of Act 2, when George arrives, with the true version of events, which Steve has finally had the opportunity to tell, in response to the news that Ann intends to marry Chris.

Joe and Chris want to spare Ann any further distress over her father's alleged guilt, so they change the subject, and avoid the issue, by suggesting a night out together as a family. Joe wants everyone to get drunk- to obliterate the need to confront uncomfortable truths. Chris admires his father ("Isn't he a great guy?") and Ann points out that this attitude is one no-one else shares - "You're the only one I know who loves his parents!". The inference is that, when Chris looks closely enough at Joe and Kate, he will find they, too, are as wrong and flawed as every other parent of every other child, and he will have to drop his admiration of them.

The Kellers' garden has a magical quality about it - part calm, part friendliness, part nostalgia - which almost ensnares George later, and Ann senses it now- "It's lovely here. The air is sweet." Again, this is ironic - the air is polluted by guilt, but it is as if an air freshener has been sprayed over it for the time being!

However, Ann knows that Kate wants her gone, because, from Kate's perspective, Ann's only reason for visiting is to formalise the wedding Kate cannot permit. We have already seen the beginnings of the tension between them, and Kate's strained efforts to keep control over the issue of Larry. Ann criticises Chris for not defending her- "you've been kind of….embarrassed". He says that both of his parents "take it for granted" that their formal engagement is as good as made. He is wrong, of course; Joe accepts it, but Kate will not.

Chris and Ann are alone on stage, and Chris explains, at length, how it feels to be a survivor from the War. This is an important scene, in two ways.

First, it focuses on one of Miller's key themes - what difference, if any, the War has made to the selfishness and the drive for personal wealth at any cost which is so typical of American citizens.

Ann complains that Chris kisses her "like Larry's brother"- as though he has lost or suppressed his own identity. He explains that he was in charge of a company of soldiers, almost all of whom died in a futile, but brave incident. Chris will have been a captain, commanding between 100 and 250 men. He explains that they were unselfish - "they killed themselves for each other". That sense of being responsible for, and to, other people, has changed him - in the heat of the war, "one new thing was made"- a sense of obligation to your colleagues in a common, dangerous cause.

Chris had hoped that their self-sacrifice would somehow "make a difference" to peacetime America, but "nobody was changed at all". He therefore feels guilty, "wrong to be alive", and the family business is, to him, "that rat-race"- not the inspiration Joe wants it to be. He is frustrated that people have not become "a little better".

He feels that, because the sacrifice of soldiers has not made peacetime America a less individualistic society- because their "monument" of death is being treated as no more significant than "a bus accident"- the peace, and all it brings, has "blood on it". That feeling of alienation has made him slow to feel entitled to a romantic relationship of his own.

Secondly, Miller concentrates on the point that neither Chris nor Ann has been quick to acknowledge the truth about their feelings for each other- it has been easier to let the situation lie unresolved, rather than confront strong feelings which will change their lives for ever. Chris will soon give up his parents in a much more violent way than he could imagine.

He has been unable, as yet, to resolve the question of Kate's obsession with Larry's survival, so that, although Ann has been "ready a long, long time", she has waited for Chris to be unambiguous about his desire to marry her and she will "never forgive" the delay.

We see from this scene that, even for the younger characters, honesty and decision-making is difficult. Chris' experiences in the war have made him emotionally reticent, slow and "ambiguous", so that he could have lost Ann, as a result of his lack of openness which he has learnt and acquired through experience - it is a social, rather than a character, flaw. This relates to Joe, and the information Miller gave about him in the stage directions at the opening of the play - Joe's lack of education makes decisions, for him, "terrible" things to have to make, but his lack of education is not his own fault. Taken out of school at the age of ten, Joe tried to educate himself at night school, but managed only one year there.

Just as Joe had told Ann "You mustn't feel that way" (about her father), so Ann now tells Chris "you mustn't feel that way any more". She asks him to lay aside his sense of guilt and shame, because (irony again) Joe was right to be paid for putting "hundreds of planes in the air" because he did not know that some would turn out to be death traps- so that "there's nothing wrong in your money". George, in Act 2, will pick up the imagery of blood – "everything they have is covered with blood". **The shamefulness of the method by which Joe has built his business for Chris is the key to the climax of the play**.

Just when Ann and Chris appear to have cleared their emotional baggage out of the way, Joe announces that her brother George is on the phone. She goes in to speak to him, but asks Chris whether they should tell Kate their marriage plans **now**. Chris puts it off "till tonight"- a decision which again defers confronting the truth. It is also necessary from a dramatic point of view, because George's revelations about what really happened in the factory - and the content of Joe's phone call with Steve - will have more power when they have the potential to affect Ann's public commitment of herself to Chris.

Ann's exit from the stage leaves it clear for Chris and Joe to have their private conversation. Joe is worried by George's phone call, because George has been to see his father that same day, and Joe sees it as an unlikely coincidence that Ann is already with them; he suspects that they may want to re-open the criminal case, "to hurt us".

The audience may feel that Joe is being too paranoid here, but his fears turn out to be entirely justified, in the sense that the truth will be extracted – and from him- in a confession of the facts in Act 2. The truth will then hurt him, fatally.

George has rung to warn Ann that their father is innocent and Joe is the guilty man; this is effectively a re-opening of the case, but in the private court of the two families, not a court of law. Steve's defence, that he is innocent, now that his own children will listen to him, mirrors Joe's legal appeal of his own innocence, and it demands that the oral evidence or testimony is re-examined. The audience does not overhear the phone call, and so does not know its content yet; we only sense Ann's agitation at what George is saying to her. She uses the frustrated exclamation "what did he say to you/tell you, for God's sake?" twice.

Joe tries to shift his thoughts from his own misgivings, to passing the business to Chris, for whom he will build a house, now that he is planning to take on the responsibility of marriage. Joe echoes Ann's insistence that "there's nothing wrong in your money", telling Chris "it's good money, there's nothing wrong with that money". While Ann believes this, genuinely, Joe knows that it is not true, but he uses other people's misconceptions to reinforce his own convenient lies.

Chris and Ann leave for a drive, so that Act 1 can end with Kate and Joe discussing George's reasons for visiting them so suddenly. Kate says that he is a practising lawyer; that he has taken a plane to see his father, after having no contact with him "all these years" since he himself went to fight in the War. She senses the danger Joe is in, and she tells him, three times, to "be smart". Neither she nor he can think of an explanation. Joe is "frightened, but angry", and the Act closes with the audience sensing that he is about to be outsmarted.

Act 1 has presented us with the Keller family, and Ann's arrival, for the perfectly innocent purpose of becoming engaged to marry Chris. Act 2 will see the arrival of George, which will be more disturbing; and Act 3 will, in a sense, present the return of Larry, via his devastating letter, and the loss of life which follows its revelation.

Act 2

Act 2 starts that evening, at twilight. Chris is sawing the broken part of Larry's tree, and he takes the branches away, leaving the "stump". This is symbolic - as night falls, Larry will no longer be a living presence; the abbreviation and the true ending of his life will be exposed. Here, it is as though, subconsciously, Chris knows that there will be no more growth on the tree, because the myth of Larry's survival is about to be torn up in a different type of storm.

Kate refers to the branches as "that thing" and says that there is more light without the tree. Again, once the lies about Larry are disposed of, the truth will come to light; it will be a relief, in some senses, even for Kate. Joe is asleep, and Kate says that he sleeps when he is worried - a reminder of the close of Act 1. Ann mistakes Joe's sleeping as a sign that he is relaxed; he is frightened and tense.

Kate stresses their vulnerability, saying that Chris must protect her and Joe, because "we're dumb.......stupid people" who "don't know anything" (by contrast, George, with his law degree, knows a great deal). Kate shares Joe's fear that the Deevers are "going to open the case again"; she threatens, dramatically, that such a crisis would kill her; and she claims, equally theatrically, that the Deever family "hates us", because Steve had maintained in court – unsuccessfully - that Joe had compelled him to ship the defective parts.

Kate uses the word "hate" three times in a few lines, and she accentuates the idea because it supports her argument that Ann must not stay, and that Chris must not pursue their relationship. George, too, will insist that the marriage should not proceed, but for a very different reason.

Ann is concerned about Kate's health, but, she says to Chris, "we're going to tell her tonight". This phrase has three simultaneous meanings - that she and Chris are going to announce their engagement; that she and George will tell her what their father has had to say about Joe's cowardice and perjury; and that she will confront Kate with the truth that Larry is dead.

Chris behaves as though he is in charge ("Just leave everything to me"…."Don't worry about it") but he is still putting off the confrontation until Kate is "in a better mood".

Ann and Sue have a conversation about marriage and about Chris. Sue remains obsessed with the financial aspects of marriage (her obsession has worn off on Jim, who, on meeting Ann, warned her that she shouldn't count her husband's money). She is dissatisfied with Jim's eagerness to please her neighbours, by fetching George from the station when he had said it was too hot to drive her to the beach.

She says that Jim spends so much time in the Kellers' house that they will charge him rent; that Chris' money "makes all the difference" to his eligibility as a marriage partner; and that the money from the factory is tainted, because "everybody knows" that Joe was guilty, really, despite his release from prison. According to Sue, people think Joe is "smart". This means that, using Kate's assessment, the people the Kellers live amongst are as stupid or dumb as they are themselves.

Jim, she says, "thinks he's in jail all the time", because she will not let him pursue his dream of being a medical researcher (he would earn a mere "twenty-five dollars a week"). She claims that Jim resents her, and that she resents living next door to the "the Holy Family"- by which, she means the Kellers' hypocritical position at the heart of their community, Chris' grand moral ideas that people should make the world a better place, and his habit of making "people want to be better than it's possible to be". Sue's view of the world is precisely the kind of cynical selfishness which Chris spoke to Ann about in Act 1; for Sue, helping others is the same as giving up your life. For Chris, social responsibility is a value which has come from seeing his soldiers sacrificing themselves - literally, giving up their lives - so that people like Sue can continue to live as they do.

Jim fought in the same battalion as Chris, and George was in the war too- so they are bound together by the same shared sense of a morality which insists that we should live our lives with integrity. Sue sneers at Jim's notion that "he feels he's compromising"; he feels diminished at having to live by her one and only principle - that life is for the acquiring of wealth.

While Sue objects to Chris' "phony idealism" because she maintains that Joe has escaped his proper punishment, and is making dirty money, Ann says that what she values in Chris is his capacity "to tell me the truth". But Chris, like his father, tells lies; he told Ann that everyone had forgotten about the legal case, to spare her discomfort and make sure she visited him. Kate comes to understand that deception, of any kind, is unacceptable – so that Joe's motives in making money for his family on the basis of lies "don't excuse it" (Act 3). Chris comes to understand that he too has been infected by the Keller lying gene, and he decides to go and live elsewhere, on his own, to cure his tendency to deceive himself and be morally weak. It is not clear whether that exile (or pilgrimage?) is still necessary after Joe's suicide.

As soon as their conversation starts, once Sue leaves, Ann attacks Chris for his habit of praising people for being better than they are; he says that Sue is "a great nurse", but she seems likely to be a perfectly ordinary one. Ann points out to Chris that Sue dislikes, "hates" and "despises" him, and she cannot understand why he pretended to her that the case "was all forgotten".

Chris did not want Ann to be persuaded, by what other people might say, to believe that Joe was guilty. Ironically, Ann has Larry's letter, so she already knows the truth - that Joe was responsible for the deaths of pilots. She demonstrates a blind faith in the legal system, because, rather like Kate's belief that Larry is still alive, she can only marry Chris if it was her own father, Steve, who made the decision to send the engine parts, knowing how dangerous they were.

Ann and Chris talk- hypothetically, for the moment - about how Chris would deal with his father's guilt, if Joe were guilty. Again, some of the language is religious (forgive, blessing, hell, crucify) and some of it is legal (suspected, wrong, innocent, falsely accused). There is an important double meaning - when Chris says "the man" who was falsely accused and put through hell is innocent, he is referring to Joe, but he should be meaning Steve.

Joe refers to himself as "dumb......I ain't brainy", and Chris calls him an "ignoramus" because he does not know the meaning of a French word. Joe senses that everyone else, including his employees, is better educated than him; his talent has lain in making a living. He calls his under-education and everyone else's over-education "a tragedy"; he does not realise that, because of his own lack of education, his own tragedy is about to take place. A little later in the scene, Chris is frustrated with Joe's "stupidity"; Joe is an even smaller man, in character and talent, than the diminished Steve Deever.

Joe does have a shrewd, cunning plan, though. He offers to find George a legal job locally, using his "very friendly" contacts, just as he offers to bring Steve back into the business, not as a partner, but to "a good job", as an employee of his. By making his potential enemies indebted or obliged to him, having done them a favour, he will minimise the risk that they will betray him - they will be complicit in his guilt. This is naïve in the extreme. Steve will not suddenly accept that he is guilty, just because he has been convicted of a crime he did not commit.

Joe presents his scheme as a way of ensuring harmony, instead of "hate" and "bitterness", when Steve is released from prison within the next year or so; he expects that Steve will go to live with Chris and Ann in their house. This is the house Joe is offering to build with money he has acquired from his betrayal of the very same Steve.

Chris refuses, saying "I don't want him in the plant"- he does not want to work somewhere tainted with corruption- as he will show, authentically, with the strongest of reactions, when he discovers what his own father has done, and he vows to leave the area, because he cannot bear to be near Joe any longer.

Faced with this current conflict, Joe falls back on empty, ritualistic language - "A father is a father" – as though it is a magic formula which confers some special status on him, or will keep him safe.

Next, we have the second of two references to Shakespeare's tragedies. Joe has already predicted to Ann that Steve, out of prison, will "come, old, mad, into your house" (like King Lear to his daughters). Now, Joe's odd little song about Lydia combing Kate's hair is reminiscent of Desdemona's "willow scene" in "Othello", where she mourns the death of her marriage in a song whilst her maid is combing her hair (Act 4 Scene 3). In tragedy, a song often precedes a decisive turn in the plot.

Jim Bayliss tells Chris that bringing George into the Kellers' territory will be bad for Kate, because she is "in bad shape", by which he means that she is emotionally unstable; he says George has "blood in his eye", meaning that he is seeking revenge, and that he has "come to take her (Ann) home." Chris declares that nobody here is afraid of George - he does not realise yet that Joe is very much afraid of George, because George brings the truth with him.

George finally arrives; he is the same age as Chris- thirty-two- and he is "on the edge of his self-restraint", because what his father has told him that day about Joe's behaviour has enraged him and provoked his sense of injustice.

George is introduced to Sue, as the woman who bought his family's former home; he is "frank" to the point of rudeness in saying that he does not want to see how she has changed it because "I liked it the way it was". We know from this remark that George is going to be a teller of the truth - rather like Priestley's Inspector Goole in "An Inspector Calls", which had its first production in the English theatre the year before Miller's play, in 1946, and also deals with post-War guilt and reconstruction.

Although he is now a lawyer, George observes that, in the real world, "there doesn't seem to be much of a law"- an allusion to its imperfectness, and the fact that a man like Joe has been able to escape justice. He has, today, started wearing his father's hat - because he is on a quest for justice for him. He says that Steve asked him to wear it. Memorably, he describes him, as Joe had done, as "little", but also as a victim - one of the "suckers"- who is shrinking so fast that in "another year there'd be nothing left but his smell". Wrongful imprisonment has deprived him of his voice, and it has wasted him away to the point of nothingness.

The confrontation which Jim told Chris George had come to seek now takes place. The repetition of words like "marry", "married", "trouble", "suckers", "smaller", "big boy", and "civilize" is like the ritual and the drawing of guns in a Wild West shoot-out, or the circling of a predator and its prey before they start a fight to the death. Chris and Ann are still trying to avoid confrontation, but they are running out of the space to keep the peace.

Chris accuses George of trying to be "the voice of God"; as a matter of fact, this - the bringing of truth - is the only function George is in the play to perform.

He explains to Ann that, having chosen to have no contact with Steve for so long, because of the crime he was convicted of, he felt that he had to tell him about Ann's engagement (to Chris); that news prompted Steve to give his version of events, which has "turned (George's) life upside down". George announces the fact of the phone call, Joe's cowardly refusal to take charge, and his direct instruction to Steve-

"He told him to weld, cover up the cracks in any way he could, and ship them out."

Joe had promised to take responsibility for this decision, had said he was ill and unable to go to the factory (the scene of the crime - so he had an alibi), and he went on to deny the phone call in court. His denial was accepted, not in the original trial, but on appeal.

This makes the Kellers the sworn enemies of the Deevers (like the warring families in Shakespeare's "Romeo and Juliet"); George challenges (and defies) Ann to "eat his food, sleep in his bed", knowing that any Keller is their enemy. He asks Ann the question which characters in this play often ask, in moments of doubt and decision-

"What're you going to do?"

George makes the same emotional appeal to Ann that Kate had done, when she implored her to remain faithful to Larry's memory - he tells her that the truth - that "Joe did it"- is what "you know in your heart". George, Chris and Ann use the word "know" twelve times in two dozen lines of dialogue. Chris is defiant; he argues (improbably) that, while his father runs an obsessively tightly controlled factory, he would delegate authority to Steve, a man so easily frightened that he would "never buy a shirt without somebody along".

Chris defends Joe by attacking Steve as a liar and a coward. Ironically, the allegations he makes here against Steve actually apply to Joe, his own father- he would "throw the blame on somebody else because he's not man enough to take it himself." This is a lie which Chris has absorbed from Joe; he does not know it from his own experience, because he has been away in the War and Steve has been in jail.

Chris asks George why he has suddenly changed his judgment, after "the court record was good enough for you all these years". George says he believed it, not because he knew the truth, but because Chris believed it. Now, he knows that his own father can and must be believed, which means that "Your Dad took everything we have"- but Ann is "one item he's not going to grab".

The dialogue, here, is full of the tension between what we **know** and what we **believe** - a linguistic link to the conversation near the start of the play where Jim criticised Frank for believing in anything, and Frank condemned Jim for not believing (in anything).

George tells Ann that Chris does know (in his heart) that the guilt is Joe's; Chris does not confirm this directly, but exclaims (bitterly? sarcastically? both?) that George is, indeed, "The Voice of God!", the bringer of the truth.

George insists that Chris is not legally and publicly a co-owner of Joe's business because it is "covered in blood", and he knows it is - he would be ashamed to be in charge of it. We know from Chris' scene with his father, just before the end of Act 1, that Joe does want to make Chris its owner, now that he is going to be a married man. At the very moment Joe intends to pass on his pride and joy to Chris, we are to find that the family business is critically defective, like the damaged goods it produced.

Chris now concedes, importantly, that he "knows" all about the business, and why Joe has retained ownership of it, but that he wants to avoid a fight because Kate is ill. We are reminded that she had said she would not survive any revealing that Joe played a part in Larry's death- and she does not yet suspect that Larry killed himself out of shame at his father's crime.

George insists that Ann must leave with him (to catch the train); Ann insists (like Chris) that he must not make a scene in front of Kate.

George does not know how determined his sister is to marry Chris, to escape her "lonely life" (as Kate calls it). He does not know that, in Larry's letter, Ann has what she believes is a trump card; she thinks that when Kate is forced to accept that Larry is dead she will stop resisting the idea of Chris marrying her.

Kate treats George like a long-lost son. She laments that "we"- the parents - "worked and planned for you", as she and Joe had done, for Larry and Chris, but that "you end up no better than us". She means that the younger generation bears the psychological scars of the War, and is as unhealthy as its parents. Chris would argue that the next generation has a moral obligation to be "better" than its parents.

Kate launches a seductive charm offensive which aims to disarm George's hostility. She reminds him that he, Chris and Frank "had big principles"- they were idealistic, and patriotic ("getting mad about Fascism"), and she brackets Chris and George together as young men who "think too much".

Now she talks about what has happened to them. Married men didn't have to enlist in the army, and so Frank had avoided being drafted into the war by marrying Lydia; now he has three children and has paid his mortgage off, although he is talentless, "a big dope". Kate tells George that he should be thinking about settling down too. She tells him to "stop being a philosopher, and look after yourself"- to set some goals for his own personal happiness, and make that his priority. Again, Kate is thinking small; just as, for Joe, the bigger world beyond the end of his garden is of no interest.

Joe has made the offer to find George a comfortable job locally, and Kate will "find you a girl and put a smile on your face". She says that George should have married Lydia; Frank, to use military language, "won the war....all the battles", by "getting into her bed". Frank's cowardice and selfishness in avoiding being called up to fight by getting married is re-shaped as a successful campaign, and something to be envied, because being married is to be envied.

We can make much the same judgment about how Joe had a similar war-time triumph, in his business at home, while others were doing the fighting in the War.

Kate returns to her theme of "hate", with which Act 2 started- she had warned Chris that people "can hate so much they'll tear the world to pieces". This is what is about to happen to the Kellers' world, but the cause of its destruction is the truth, not hatred. Ann stresses in Act 3 that she means no harm to Joe and Kate, and she means it.

Kate wants to avoid "an argument" (she uses the word three times, while she strokes George's hair in a gesture of soothing and "desperation") by finding common ground; she says "We all got hit by the same lightning", but this is untrue, because the Deever family are victims, not of the war, but of Joe's selfish, weak, exploitative behaviour.

She goes on to tell George "you don't hate us", and asks him why he pretends "to hate us", twice. This contrasts with the language of love - Kate has just said to George, "I told you you loved that girl" (Lydia), and Chris backed her up with an ironic quotation from the Bible, about self-sacrifice- "And truer love hath no man!".

He means two things by this comment - that the male drive to love and settle down with a woman is integral to masculinity (he is about to commit himself publicly to Ann); and that Frank has "won the war" because he avoided the sacrifice of dying for his country. The reference is to St John 15:13 in the New Testament-

"Greater love hath no man than this, that a man lay down his life for his friends". Remember that Chris has witnessed at first hand just this kind of self-sacrifice, by the soldiers he commanded.

Joe reappears, and he knows why George had come, because he has been watching the scene, from just inside the kitchen door, ever since Jim told Chris why George has come. Joe approaches George "rapidly.......with strained joviality", and the laughter over Kate's match-making stops abruptly, because what we might call the shoot-out is about to begin.

Joe's conversation with George is serious, immediately; they will not allow Chris to interrupt and deflect them from what we may call a duel of conscience. Joe's factory is large and successful. Steve is ill, not because of a heart complaint, but because "his soul" is suffering. Joe describes him insultingly, to George, as "a little man", but he still repeats to George the placatory offer of a job for Steve which he had already made to Ann in Act 2. George points out that his father "hates your guts, Joe", and that this is precisely what Joe should "expect him to think of you". Remember that Joe has just seen George tell Ann that he - Joe- "destroyed our family". He still denies the truth, but gives George his well-rehearsed, brass-necked version of Steve as a man who "never learned to take the blame", illustrated by two examples, one of them from 1937 - ten years previously.

It is ironic that Joe should preach to anyone on the issue of taking the blame, and particularly that a comment he aims at Steve applies so accurately to himself - "There are certain men in the world who rather see everybody hung before they'll take the blame".

The tension drops, because Joe thinks he has convinced George about his father's lack of character. George agrees to stay for the evening, which means he is now to be included in the Keller conspiracy. Chris offers him a clean shirt, and a date with a girl called Charlotte Tanner, whom they propose to telephone immediately. George is (briefly) seduced by "the whole atmosphere" of the two families' long interconnection. It seems that the Keller charm may just be working one more time.

Now, Joe and Kate let their guard drop, because they think they have dealt with the threat George has brought. Joe tells George that he is "amazingly the same" because he is never ill, and Kate confirms **he has never been ill in bed for fifteen years** - which amounts a confession that his "illness" on the day the engine parts were shipped was a cowardly pretence, a deliberate deception. George is alert to the lie. He puts the key question, directly- "What happened that day, Joe?"

At this moment of high drama the comical Frank arrives, with Larry's horoscope. The scene which follows is short, but it heightens the tension, by delaying Joe's inevitable confession of the truth. Charlotte Tanner - who symbolises the temptation of condoning the Keller lies - is on the phone, waiting for George to ask her out, but George is transfixed by the knowledge that Joe has "never been sick….he simply told (Steve Deever) to kill pilots, and covered himself in bed!"

Frank's interest in horoscopes derives from his luck in avoiding being drafted into the army, purely because of his date of birth and his status as a married man. He claims to have found out that Larry has the same sort of cosmic luck - that he cannot have died on November 25th because it is his "favourable day", the day "everything good was shining on". The superstition seems ridiculous, and almost farcical, in the context of the unfolding drama;

but Frank asks, rhetorically, "Is it junk to feel that there's a greater power than ourselves?".

For Miller, the audience, and - finally- the characters, there will indeed be evidence of a greater power - not the power of luck, but the power of the truth, which Joe, Kate and Chris have all tried to suppress and bury, but which cannot be kept buried once Larry speaks from beyond the grave.

The taxi arrives. Both Kate and George want Ann to leave with him; Chris does not, because his future happiness is at stake if she walks away now. She sides with Chris, and sends George on his way. Chris, agitated, has implored them all to say "nothing more……..about the case or Larry………till Christ comes". This is the language of religion again; the second coming of Christ is the day of revelation and divine judgment, and it is closer than they think.

Chris and Kate argue bitterly over her decision to pack Ann's bag (they throw the phrase back and forth five times in fifteen lines or so). Kate rejects Ann because "she doesn't belong here"; Chris tells his mother that, if she rejects Ann, he will leave too, which is the last thing Joe wants. He intervenes "cruelly" and criticises

Kate for losing her senses and "talking like a maniac"- an insult, and loose talk, for which she hits him, violently. She insists - fired up by Frank's horoscope - that Larry is "coming back, and everyone has got to wait.....till he comes; forever and ever till he comes". This is treating Larry as a Christ-like figure, and Kate is echoing the language of the Lord's Prayer ("thine is the kingdom, the power and the glory, for ever and ever. Amen"). Everyone except Kate knows that Larry is never coming back.

She and Chris have an emotionally charged exchange, based on the words "dead", "alive", "killed", and, especially, the phrase "(never) let him go". Chris means, by "him", Larry - he wants Kate to concede that Larry is dead so that she accepts that he can legitimately marry Ann. Kate points out that if Chris lets Larry go, he must then also "let your father go", because *if they accept that Larry is dead they must accept that Joe was responsible for his death*. For Kate, this is inconceivable, because "God does not let a son be killed by his father". This is her mantra, her reassuring comfort blanket - her equivalent of Joe's motto "a father is a father".

Kate goes into the house, leaving Joe and Chris on stage. Joe tries to dismiss what she has just said on the grounds that she is insane ("she's out of her mind"), but Chris will not be deflected from the reflection/accusation. He says to Joe "you did it" three times; Joe responds, three times, demanding "what's the matter with you?".

The central word "kill" occurs five times, in six lines of dialogue, along with one use of "murdered". Chris continues to interrogate Joe, like a prosecutor, repeating the question "What did you do?" three times.

Joe's defence is in the form of another repeated question- "what could I do?". Joe had said, of Steve, that the justice system punishes a mistake by hanging you by the thumbs; now, he accuses Chris of wanting to hang him. He maintains that he did not kill anyone ("How could I kill anybody?"), and that he was protecting the "business"- he uses the word five times.

He was actually trying to protect his own forty years of work (and his reputation). When he justifies his actions by telling Chris "I did it for you"- because he intended the business to pass to him (and, presumably, to Larry too) - it is a sentiment we find both noble and pathetic, because there is self-interest at work here, as well as the desire "to make something" for his children. Joe's fatal decision was not entirely selfish, but it was wrapped up with his own sense of his personal identity; the factory is a symbol of his value in the world, and he sees it almost as an extension or a reflection of himself.

Joe defends himself-weakly- by saying that he "thought" the engine parts would not be used, and "thought" he could resolve the issue later; he intended to tell the authorities, but the planes flew and crashed before he got round to it. He has, in fact, never stopped thinking about it since.

Chris concentrates on what Joe "knew"- he knew that the planes were unsafe. While Chris and his men were "dying" in combat, Joe too was "killing" his comrades. He spits out the word "business" contemptuously, three times, in the closing speech of the Act; the business, which is so central to Joe's self-image and his sense of purpose, is irrelevant to Chris.

Act 3

At the end of Act 2, the truth about the criminal case has emerged, and everyone has acknowledged it - Joe, Kate, Chris, Steve, Ann, George.

Act 3, therefore, deals with the consequences, and reveals the further truth that **Larry chose to die out of shame at his father's responsibility** for the fatal engines. Joe has no option but to redefine his relationship with his biological sons, and with "all his sons". Miller does not take up unnecessary time here- Act 3 is only 15% of the play as a whole.

The outcome of the play hinges on the clash between Chris' demands and his parents' pragmatism. He argues that "you" (his parents) "can be better", and he judges that "there's a universe of people outside and you're responsible to it". This takes us back to what he had told Ann about his experiences in the war, and his belief that the sense of responsibility soldiers showed there to each other needs to be marked with a statue or a monument, to remind people of it. Joe and Kate, on the other hand, believe that patriotism is all very well, but we have our lives to live, in our families. To Joe, "Nothin' is bigger" than "the family"; Kate says that, for Chris, that is not so, and that Joe's motivation - to provide money for his family - is not enough - "it don't excuse it that you did it for the family".

Act 3 begins with a conversation between Kate and Jim, which Miller uses to give us the image of a star - not, now, the stars of horoscopes, but "the star of one's honesty". Jim says that Chris has gone off to "watch his star go out", in the sense that Chris now knows that he has not been honest with himself regarding the doubts he always had at the back of his mind over Joe's innocence.

Jim, too, has "compromised", by living the life Sue has chosen for him, rather than doing the research which would make him "better". Chris has gone away to consider what should be done with Joe. He concludes that sending him to prison will not achieve anything ("Do I raise the dead when I put him behind bars?"). He accuses himself of cowardice ("I suspected my father and I did nothing about it"), and he has decided to leave, without Ann, for another part of the country - forfeiting his own financial security and prospects of happiness as a form of punishment which he imposes on himself. In judging that he has become "practical" like his parents (we would use the word "pragmatic"),

Chris has turned into a less good person than he could have been, so the star of his honesty has gone out.

Jim judges that, while he and Kate - older people- can tolerate being dishonest with themselves, Chris will find it harder to deal with (because he has a social conscience which goes beyond the duty merely to protect your own family). He is right; just as Chris will punish himself for what he sees as his own cowardice, he will judge that Joe, once it is clear that he is responsible for Larry's suicide, has no place in the civilised world ("Now tell me where you belong").

Jim leaves, and Kate and Joe have their last private conversation. She warns him, ominously, that "this thing is not over yet", and that he needs to be "smart" (which we know he is not) and to "figure out your life". Kate fears that they no longer know their son ("they say in the war he was such a killer"). She herself is worn out; she has "no strength to think any more", and therefore she cannot suggest to Joe how he can stabilise this emotionally charged atmosphere. We have seen throughout the play that Joe does not know how to defuse emotional bombs or deal with strong feelings in other people.

Joe's weak defence, that we are all less than perfect - "A man can't be a Jesus in this world"- and his inability to come to terms with the concept that he needs to seek to be "forgiven", puts him firmly in the category of "little men". He asks Kate to do his thinking for him ("what do I do? Tell me, talk to me, what do I do?"), and, later, he asks Chris "what do you want me to do? .... What should I want to do?"

Jim "knows" about Joe's guilt. Ann "knows". Chris knows. The question is, how can Joe atone for it? Kate thinks that if Joe makes it plain to Chris that he is willing to "pay for what you did" by going to prison, Chris might forgive him, and "wouldn't ask you to go". This is exactly how Chris does react, until the worst possible news - the real reason for Larry's death by suicide - emerges; at that point, it is no longer possible for Joe not to go away from his family, because the killing of a son by a father is beyond the pale, or, as Kate had put it in Act 2, something God does not permit.

Joe laments Chris' morality; he praises Larry instead, for his philosophy that the wider, outside world finishes at the end of your garden. Joe cannot understand the concept of wider social responsibility until he reads Larry's suicide letter. Because Joe would forgive anything Chris did wrong, he expects to be forgiven himself, purely "because I'm his father and he's my son". Chris, though, expects his father to behave responsibly ("I know you're no worse than most men but I thought you were better"), and therefore cannot forgive him for killing his brother. Joe foreshadows the end of the play when he says that "if there's something bigger than" the family connection - the dimension of responsibility to "all my sons" - "I'll put a bullet in my head".

Joe is beginning to be resourceless - he "slumps" on a chair. Kate tries to reassure him that "nothing is going to happen". How wrong can she be?

Joe starts to talk about himself in the past tense, as if he is already dead - "that's all I ever lived for"; he will go on to tell Chris "I'm a dead man, I'm an old dead man", just before he goes into the house, from which he will not emerge again alive.

Ann has spent the whole evening in her bedroom, deciding what to do with Larry's letter. She is determined to use it to prove to Kate that Larry is dead, so that she can "let him go" and let her marry Chris. This is the last twist in the plot, because only Ann knows of the letter - the audience and the other characters do not.

Ann opens their discussion in a soothing and non-confrontational way, as far as that is possible, by telling Kate that she is "not going to do anything about" the "something I want to tell you". It is only at the end of the play that we understand what she means - she has no desire to see Joe punished for his deceit, his dishonest release from prison, and for causing his own son to kill himself. She only wants to use the letter to persuade Kate that her marriage to Chris can and must proceed. That will mean that Kate stops crippling Chris emotionally, and making him feel guilty, and that she will "set him free" to be the husband Ann wants him to be capable of being- a "better" person.

Joe agrees, because Ann has power over his own fate. Ann tells Kate "you had two sons. But you've only got one now". This echoes what Joe had said to Lydia very early in Act 1- "I had two sons, now I got one". Soon, he will have to admit that the twenty-one other pilots whose deaths he caused were "all my sons".

Kate still refuses to do as Ann asks. Coldly, she wants Ann to have a "lonely life". Perhaps

Frank's horoscope has breathed new life into her surreal dream that Larry is still alive. She challenges Ann to tell her how he died, and both she and Ann send Joe inside the house; Ann wants to spare him the revelation she is about to make to Kate.

Ann stresses that she has no desire to avenge her family against the Kellers; she had always believed that Joe was innocent, and she simply wants to marry Chris, to put an end to being "so lonely". Kate's obstinacy over Larry means that *only the written record will force her to face the truth*.

While Kate is reading the letter, Chris reappears. He says that he thought Ann would have left; he means that he expected her to reject him because of Joe's lies and cowardice, so far as they are now (incompletely) known about. In his moral code, there is nothing wrong with being lonely, but there is now a great deal wrong with having Joe as your father-in-law.

Chris himself cannot bear to be near him, and he rejects Kate as well, for infecting him with their cowardice. Because he no longer respects himself ("I spit on myself") he is going into a self-imposed exile - without Ann. To Chris, Ann's knowledge about Joe's perjury and cowardice will create an impossible obstacle "in your heart". Chris had complained, in Act 1, that "every time I reach out for something I want, I have to pull back because other people will suffer". Here, he seems to be judging that Ann will suffer, even though she says she will not; he is imposing his morality on her, and he will soon - and finally - impose it on his father as well.

Joe comes out of the house, seeking to make peace with Chris, but he receives his judgment instead. Joe behaves in his usual placatory way, telling Chris to "burn" the money from the business "if it's dirty"; he wants to preserve the father-son relationship at any cost. He wants to please Chris, so he asks him "what do you want me to do?".

Chris points out that Joe has to decide for himself; the difficulty is that Joe does not have a conscience, or an education, or a feeling of social responsibility, so he cannot easily arrive at the right thing to do, or indeed often arrive at any decision at all.

Joe offers to go to prison - the solution Chris has already rejected as pointless - but he still tries to justify himself, as being no more corrupt than any other supplier to the army during the

War. Chris concedes that that is a valid argument. Chris has "nothing to say" to Joe, and finds his presence provocative, because he has failed to be "better" than he is. He is bad because he is not good enough.

Ann wants Chris to see Larry's letter. This is her last desperate move to persuade him that he need not feel guilty and crippled about marrying "Larry's girl", whatever Kate may say. As Chris starts to read it, Kate (who knows its contents) warns Joe to "go away"; even before this terrible new information, Chris has said that, if Joe tries to get close to him, he will "hurt" him.

Kate pleads with Chris not to tell Joe what is in the letter. She is thinking of Joe's remark that, if there is something bigger than the father-son relationship, and he loses that, he will put a bullet in his head; she knows what is about to happen, although Sue was being sarcastic when she had described Kate as "psychic" earlier.

The change in Chris's position towards Joe comes in his language; instead of leaving Joe to do "what you want to do", he demands "Now you tell me what you must do........now tell me where you belong". The answer, and Chris' meaning, is clear - Joe, having induced Larry's suicide, does not belong in society at all.

Chris reads the letter out aloud, less for Joe's benefit than for the audience's. The key words are Larry's remark that "I can't bear to live any more". Chris challenges Joe to continue to "blame the world" for his cowardly behaviour. Larry has made that position untenable, by making it clear that he was about to kill himself because he was so ashamed of what Joe has done.

Joe's calm and quiet response suggests, at first, that he knows he must go to prison (for manslaughter as well as criminal negligence and perjury). He must go into exile, to atone for his deficiencies, just as Chris has decided to - only Joe's faults are on a cosmic scale, because no father is allowed to kill his son, in the world of the Kellers.

Joe tells Kate that he realises now that, to Larry, the pilots "were all my sons......I guess they were". This means that he has to accept that he is an accidental mass murderer as well as the cause of his own son's suicide. Keller by name, killer by nature.

In the brief moments after Joe has gone inside, and before the gunshot is heard, the audience knows what to expect, because of the foreshadowing we have noted in this commentary.

Chris says that "Nobody could stop him now"- not from going to prison, but from finally doing something brave and true. Kate says that "the war is over!"; she is referring not to the Second World War, but to the war within the Keller family, and the war between truth and lies, secrets and what is out in the open, rumour and fact, fantasy and reality.

Chris tells Kate that what Joe has done is far too serious to be atoned for by being "sorry". It can only be atoned for by grasping the tragic knowledge that there is, after all, something "bigger than the family" - the wider world - and taking responsibility for the implications of your offences against the world, even if they were done in defence of your family.

If we accept Miller's argument that Joe is a tragic hero, then by the standards of that genre Joe's suicide is necessary and proportionate. However, it can also be seen as a cowardly and pathetic gesture by a spineless man. As soon as she knows her husband is dead, Kate tells Chris that he can finally cast off the shadow of his inadequate father, and go on to "live" because of the deaths of Larry and Joe, both of which are finally acknowledged and accepted.

Characters

How many characters are there in the play?

You may be tempted to stop at nine (Joe, Kate, Chris, Ann, George, Jim, Sue, Frank, Lydia), or ten if you include the boy Bert, who appears briefly, twice. But you might, having thought about that question a little more, add two more characters - Larry Keller and Steve Deever.

Larry Keller is dead, but he "appears", with a devastating impact, at the end of the play, because his letter gives him a critical voice (we could even say that he is the true "voice of God" in Act 3 of the play).

Steve Deever is in prison, but when he finally has the chance to tell George the truth, he becomes an important character, because his truth exposes Joe's fictional account of events. Joe has betrayed Steve, and Steve is a silent character in the background of the play, but a powerful one, because he is still paying the price of that betrayal. The consequences of Joe Keller's lies affect the lives of the living, every day, as well as being a betrayal of the dead pilots- other people's sons.

The Keller family

Ann says that "people like to do things for the Kellers". They are friendly, likeable, and, on the surface, both successful and welcoming. But they dislike intrusion, because they need to protect the secret of the shame which should attach to Joe's behaviour during the War.

Kate and Joe work very hard to maintain the lie that Steve Deever, not Joe, was responsible for the decision which led to the deaths of twenty-one pilots; but even they do not know that their own son Larry committed suicide as a consequence of his father's role in the scandal, until Ann proves it to them at the end of the play.

The Kellers appear to have achieved the American Dream of material success through hard work. They appear to be patriotic, because one son (Larry) is missing in action and the other (Chris) was a captain in the Army. But they are compromised, because their money is "dirty" and steeped in "blood". Their neighbours sense this, but nobody can prove it. Joe was acquitted of any crime, on appeal, while Steve Deever was found responsible, and remains in prison.

The Deever children, Ann and George, have cut themselves off from their father, because they believe he is guilty. It is only Ann's strong desire to marry Chris Keller that changes the outlook; George hears the real story from his father, and seeks to prevent Ann's marriage, because marrying Chris would be sleeping with the enemy; the Kellers' deception has destroyed the Deever family.

Kate Keller opposes the marriage for different reasons - allowing it to proceed would be to acknowledge that Larry is dead, and, because Larry was a pilot, admitting that he is dead will be the same as admitting Joe's guilt and responsibility for the crime which, Kate says, God does not allow - the killing of a son by his father.

Joe had managed to deny, in court, the verbal or oral evidence of his crucial telephone call to Steve at the factory. Ann has Larry's suicide note; the Kellers cannot ignore, or deny, this written testimony. That note forces Joe, finally, to take responsibility and therefore to take his own life.

The Keller family has a symbolic value as the kind of family Americans admire for their enterprise. Miller felt that many people had profited improperly from the War, as the Kellers clearly have. The quality of loyalty to your own family is admirable, up to a point; but Joe takes it too far, by using it to justify his own weaknesses of selfishness, social irresponsibility and greed. His own wife eventually tells him that his motive- to provide for his family- does not excuse his actions.

Miller uses the character of Chris Keller to explore the guilt of the survivor and to argue that if the War was worth fighting, then the peace must usher in an age of greater social cohesion and less individualism. The older Kellers (like the Birling parents in JB Priestley's "An Inspector Calls") stand in the way of this need to be "better", because they are morally bankrupt, stuck in the old ways of living, and unable to make the huge shift society requires.

This is why Joe must die; although he is a "little man", he is a tragic hero, because he can no longer, in the end, ignore his responsibility for the manslaughter of pilots and the death of his own son. The manner in which he accepts it goes some way towards redeeming him, but he still has to die, because otherwise the world of human behaviour would be a sub-human "zoo".

Miller criticises Joe and his family for their lack of interest in the wider world beyond the building line of their own house and plot - they have no time for newspapers, or books. Miller defends them, too, as uneducated people: Joe only has the common sense of a peasant to guide him, so it is not surprising that he makes fatally bad decisions. Kate is over-emotional, and superstitious; her lack of education makes her irrational, and makes her judgments faulty, too. Chris has been in the wider world, and so he has developed a sense of what is possible and necessary, if a society is to enforce proper standards of behaviour from its citizens. He cannot bear the sight of his father, once he realises what he has done.

Sue Bayliss refers to the Kellers, sarcastically, as "the Holy family". She objects to Chris' "phony idealism". Her pragmatism - her obsessive demand for money from her husband - goes too far, but she is right to sense that the Kellers are not as good as they say and think they are, and that there is something deeply wrong, but unexposed, about them.

The Kellers - and Sue Bayliss - symbolise the perversion of individualism in post-War America.

Frank Lubey avoided the draft, and so he has an enviable domestic life, and owns his house outright. By being less patriotic, he has "won the war"; he is settled and happy, though directionless and "a big dope", according to Kate. Miller uses Frank and Lydia Lubey to show the Kellers, Sue Bayliss, and the Deevers that there is more to life than compulsive industry and the pursuit of wealth - if only they will see it for themselves.

By putting the Keller family under the spotlight, Miller makes the point that we cannot keep our house in order by ignoring the demands of morality. Lies and secrets will be uncovered, sooner or later.

The Kellers may be good, pleasant neighbours, but they have been extremely bad citizens. Joe has been so bad that he decides to sacrifice his own life to show that he finally recognises how much wrong he has done, to his own son, and to other people's - to "All My Sons".

Joe Keller

Miller describes him precisely at the start of the play; he is in his late fifties ("nearing sixty"), heavily built and slow of mind; deliberate in thought and deed; educated only to a basic level (he tells us that he spent one year at night school); he makes decisions without genuine intelligence or insight, but by trawling through his own past experience and drawing on his "peasant-like common sense". This helps to explain why he made the wrong decision over the faulty engine parts.

In Act 3, Keller says he is sixty-one (an apparent contradiction of the age Miller has given him in the opening stage direction), and that he was "put out" by his own family at the age of ten. His business goes back forty years.

He is a man of solid and limited values and visions. He has worked hard, to meet Kate's demands ("you wanted money, so I made money") and his business career is based on dogged determination. He would have been born in 1886, and so aged forty-three at the time of the Wall Street Crash; his business survived a crisis in 1937 and, again, during the War, when the production process was faulty. Joe was imprisoned, then released on appeal, and he spent the next fourteen months making his factory bigger and better than before, and restoring his reputation, to the point where he became "a respected man again; bigger than ever".

Joe cannot think for himself; he often asks Kate or Chris what he should do. He tries to placate other people, but there is a confrontational and brass-necked undercurrent, when it comes to protecting his business interests. His accusations that Steve Deever is weak and cowardly are detailed and well-rehearsed, and he relates them smoothly to George. These lies are uncomfortable for the audience to hear, because we know that the criticisms Joe makes of Steve ironically apply to him instead. Joe and Kate have constructed a careful (and increasingly unsustainable) web of lies; they are finally caught out when Joe, arrogantly, claims that his success in business is because "I ain't got time to get sick", and Kate confirms the truth - "he hasn't been laid up in fifteen years".

Joe is sick of his wife's superstitions; he agrees with Chris that it is wrong to let her continue to pretend that Larry will come home alive, but he has allowed the deception to continue because it is easier to do that than to tell the uncomfortable truth. His weakness and lack of courage here reflect exactly the decision-making process by which he did the wrong thing with the engine parts.

Miller is skilful in giving us the sense that Joe has an obvious need to lie, and is such an experienced liar that he now believes in the alternative version of events he has invented. However, while he accommodates Kate's fantasies about Larry being still alive, on a deeper level he also has a psychological need for the truth about the faulty parts to come out, although he is terrified of the consequences.

Joe desperately seeks the approval of his wife and his son. He has real difficulty in reading Chris' temperament, because the moral dimension in Chris' behaviour - his "idealism"- is so alien to Joe.

He remarks to Kate, with some bitterness, that "Larry….. was a boy we lost…he understood the way the world is made", while Chris is problematic, because "He don't understand money". Joe has not been quite ready to hand the business over to Chris, but the threat of losing it is less disturbing to him than the threat of being alienated from Chris - he will do anything to avoid that. His dream is not so much of a long and happy retirement with Kate as of facilitating a happy life for Chris, who will live with Ann in a biggish house, and run the factory - like father, like son.

Joe tells Kate "I'm his father and he's my son, and if there's something bigger than that I'll put a bullet in my head!". There is something bigger- society- and so he does.

Kate Keller

Miller provides a short analysis of her, when she makes her delayed appearance in Act 1- she is "in her early fifties, a woman of uncontrolled inspirations, and an overwhelming capacity for love".

She is maternal, and people tend to tell her their deepest feelings. She insists that Anne must obey "her heart", but what she presents as deep, instinctive truths is often really just wishful thinking.

She remains deeply attached to, and interested in, everyone in the neighbourhood, past and present; she is interested in whether or not Ann's parents will live together when Steve is released from prison. She treats George as a long-lost son, and wants to fix him up with a pleasant girl - although her motivation here is complicated by the fact that keeping George on side will help to keep the Keller secrets secret.

She is suffering from an unspecified illness; she has continual insomnia and headaches, and Dr Jim says she should not be having late sleepless nights, because they do her no good. He warns that a confrontation involving George is potentially damaging for her fragile health. She is under psychological pressure, maintaining the myth that Larry is still alive, partly to avoid the grief of a mother, but also in order to continue to keep Joe's secrets. The illness may be a physical expression of the strain she feels over the central issue of conscience - that if she concedes that Larry is dead, she admits that Joe is responsible for his death, and this is one of the "certain things" which "can never be" admitted and which "can never happen".

Miller wrote (in his "Introduction to the Collected Plays") that Kate and her superstitions originally had a more prominent role in the play, but this became less important as the relationship between Joe and Chris became more significant. In his autobiography, "Timebends", Miller claims that Kate has a "wish to take vengeance on (Joe) by driving him psychically to his knees and ultimately to suicide".

This seems rather odd, because Kate's behaviour in the play always serves to deflect Joe from the threat of the truth; she repeatedly moves him out of the way of conversations which could distress him. Finally, she says that she has "no strength to think any more"- her span of control, over Chris, over Ann, over George, has become weak.

If Miller intends Kate to drive Joe to kill himself, I think he has failed. Rather, she says that she can no longer shield Joe from the final truth about Larry. As a consequence, she has to leave Joe to face the consequences of his actions alone.

Chris Keller

His mother says that he has a reputation as a "killer" in the war; he was in charge of a company of soldiers, most of whom died, bravely ("they didn't die; they killed themselves for each other"). The war has changed him; even his parents sense that. He explains to Ann that the comradeship in the Army engendered a new sense of responsibility, which has shifted his focus in life significantly. He measures his own achievement on a moral scale, not just by counting the money he has. His standards are more exacting than Joe, in particular, is used to. Chris challenges or inspires people (like Jim) to do something in their lives to help others; to Sue, this is "phony idealism", from someone who is a member of the "Holy Family".

Chris interrogates Joe near the end of the play, and he puts him under intense pressure to confess what he really did during the crisis over the defective production process (Chris' demand for the truth is, for Joe, like being hung by your thumbs). The answer - that he was wholly responsible, and is not innocent at all - leads Chris to a moral dilemma. Kate tells Joe that he must do what he has to, to make Chris **forgive** him. Joe insists that "a man can't be a Jesus in this world", but this is precisely what

Chris does demand, with his talk of how his parents can and should be "better".

Chris decides that to imprison Joe would serve no purpose. The phrase he uses is very interesting - "Do I raise the dead when I put him behind bars?"- because, in the Gospels, Christ raises Lazarus from the dead. Chris decides that he will himself go into exile, give up Ann, and live elsewhere, by himself, to purge himself of his infection with the Keller cowardice, and the self-deception over Joe's guilt which he has indulged, against his better judgment, for so long.

Then Larry's suicide note makes Joe's crimes worse - they are not just negligence, multiple manslaughter, lying in court, and using Steve as a scapegoat, but causing Larry's death too. It is Chris who makes the decision that Joe cannot stay at home once Larry's death is added to the charge sheet; and Joe chooses suicide rather than prison.

Chris' name is close to "Christ" (just as Keller is close to killer), and he behaves like a confessor or a priest, in his self-denial and his concern for the appropriate punishment and atonement for sin, and his evangelical devotion to the idea that it is the duty of every person to live a morally upright life. While Joe is a killer who lies, Chris is the killer of lies. He calls himself "a pretty tough guy"- he will not allow himself, or others, to fall short of his own exacting, or tough, standards.

He uses Biblical language again, when he, Kate and George discuss marriage- "And truer love hath no man!". The discussion is about the true romantic love men feel for women (as George used to, for Lydia, before he went to the War, leaving her to marry Frank), but Chris, uniquely, is very aware of the (unromantic and sacrificial) "love a man can have for a man" in the combat zone. The love Chris feels is always truer, purer, deeper and more demanding than other people's, because it is a moral love. He tells Ann "I love you. I love you a great deal"- we should note the intensity and weight of this. It is not something Joe would say to Kate, or Kate to Joe.

Chris often talks about human life as if it were lived by animals (the land of the great big dogs, a zoo, the rat-race, an elephant, a frightened mouse, a Russian wolfhound, a gorilla, you're not even an animal, the cats in that alley). He differentiates human behaviour from animal behaviour less than the other characters.

In Act 2, Chris tries to defend his family against the accusations George brings with him, questioning his right to speak as "the voice of God". In Act 3, Chris himself takes on the role George had in Act 2, as he, in turn, becomes the judge and jury at the informal trial, in his own back garden, of Joe's morality; Chris is on stage throughout the last part of the play.

Chris is aged thirty-two (so is Frank, who, however, avoided being enlisted for the war) and five years older than his dead brother Larry. Larry's death, and the deaths of the men Chris was in charge of, himself, have changed him. He is not materialistic; he is not interested in his standard of living, but in the quality of his living. He is impatient, and even threatens George and Joe with violence; Kate knows that he acquired a reputation as "such a killer" in the war. We should take this as a sign that - unlike Jim, and Joe - he will not compromise with the truth; when he finds a lie, he will kill it, and his idealism cannot come to terms, or compromise, with his father's complete lack of idealism.

Jim and Sue Bayliss

Jim is a doctor; his wife used to be a nurse. He would like to do medical research, to find cures for illnesses, but she insists that he must make calls on patients, even on Sunday mornings, for more money. She is driven by the notion that the right thing is for the husband to provide for his family - rather like Joe feels Kate believes, but more so. Jim had once gone to New Orleans to do research, and he was poor but happy there. Sue came to fetch him back to Ohio. She will not let him follow his dream. She is a dumpy, overweight, middle-aged woman who denies him the right to dream, and forces him to compromise, so that he has come to believe that men's "star" goes out - they all have to compromise, and give up, for their family, the things which matter to them most. They are browbeaten into giving up being honest about what they want to achieve.

He is disappointed with the life he has. He appears at the start of Act 3 after making a house call after one o'clock in the morning. He admires Ann's "intelligence", but, if his reaction is similar to the other men's, he means, really, her attractiveness. He is bored, and would welcome the sight of a pretty girl in the neighbourhood. He is friendly with Kate. We could imagine him leaving Sue, out of frustration, in order to achieve a happier way of life with a less materialistic woman. This is very much what Ann represents, for Chris.

He tells Kate that he has **always known** about Joe's guilt, and that Steve Deever was innocent; it **occurred to** him **a long time ago**. As a doctor, he is used to diagnosing illness; he can see that all is not right with the Kellers.

The Kellers have lost a son; the Baylisses have lost real intimacy and any shared vision they may once have had. When Joe tries to defend his actions by saying that Kate had wanted money, the audience feels that he is comparing her (unfairly) with the woman next door. Kate is a warmer person than Sue, and she would never encourage Joe to do the wrong thing for financial gain.

Ann Deever

Ann and Chris both want to be married. Chris has a grand, warm, dreamy vision of a "beautiful" domestic life, and he "thinks of Annie" because he knows her best, from their childhood, when she was, literally, the girl next door. He has had little experience of women, and the background they share holds out the prospect of a lasting relationship, for him. For her, Chris is "somebody to tell me the truth"- she does not care about his family wealth. She expects Chris to confide in her any doubts he has about his father's innocence; she infers to Chris, in Act 2, via incomplete sentences, that she would be unable to marry him if Joe turns out to have been a murderer after all. Miller cannot have her say this clearly and openly, because she has the evidence throughout the play (in Larry's letter) that Joe is indeed a murderer.

Ann has always known that Larry is dead, because she has his suicide letter. She has no wish to harm Kate, and no grudge against the Keller family, because she accepts the legal ruling which condemned her father for the crime. Ann has rejected her own father on the grounds that he had behaved immorally, and she cut herself off from him from the moment when the death of Larry was reported - "Father or no father, there's only one way to look at him". This clear-sighted morality foreshadows the need for Chris to do the same to Joe at the end of the play.

She is twenty-six, and has been living in New York for three and a half years (Kate says). She and Chris have been writing to each other, but they have not seen each other for five years.

Miller's stage direction, when Ann appears, eventually, more than half way through Act 1, tells us that she is determined – "capable of holding fast to what she knows". She sends George away, after resisting his demands that she leaves with him.

She is described as "a beauty" (Kate); "the prettiest" (Chris); Joe admires her legs. But there is more to her than a superficial attractiveness. She is more determined to marry Chris than Kate is to prevent her from doing so, although she nearly abandons her mission in Act 1. She claims to be "not very good in an argument", and she doggedly tries to "settle Larry" in Kate's mind, without a confrontation.

Ann is determined that she will not be "going out of here alone"; her visit aims to "free" Chris from his "embarrassment" over Larry, by establishing once and for all that she is not spoken for as Larry's betrothed. Even in Act 1, she is - calmly- trying to open Kate's closed mind-

"MOTHER   What your father did had nothing to do with Larry. Nothing.

ANN   But we can't know that."

Very little deflects or interests Ann, apart from her mission to marry Chris. If you go through the play and look at her speeches, most of them are half a dozen words long, at most- she co-ordinates other people's conversation, but offers little in the way of judgments, except to defend Chris against Sue's accusation that he is too idealistic.

At the start of Act 3, she has to assert herself ("Larry is dead, Kate"). It is only when Kate grasps her wrists and hurts her that she is driven to produce Larry's letter, which seals the tragedy. Before she does so, she tells Joe to go inside - she wants to protect him from the revelation it contains. Chris will not allow her to go with him into his self-chosen exile. Once she has given him the letter to read, she has no more lines to speak; when the shot is heard, Chris sends her to fetch Jim. Miller leaves it unclear whether or not Joe's suicide will enable them to marry, after all.

The fact that Ann has Larry's letter makes her vital to the plot. Miller motivates her behaviour convincingly, but she, Chris, Larry and George are all much less three-dimensional than Kate and Joe; the play is their tragedy, not the Deevers'.

George Deever

Just as Miller surrounded Ann with suspense, and made her intriguing by delaying her appearance in Act 1, he delays the appearance of George until Act 2 is well underway, although his arrival was imminent at the end of Act 1. The tension grows, too, because Jim says that George is looking for a confrontation, and has come to take Ann home with him.

Miller's stage direction tells us, rather oddly, that George is "on the edge of his self-restraint" and is afraid he may start to shout; he is extremely agitated because he knows his father is innocent, and because of the necessary consequence of that knowledge; that, to Ann, the Kellers are - or should be - an untouchable enemy.

He explains to Ann that what he knows now has turned his life upside down - an ironic reference to what is about to happen to the Kellers' lives, too.

He says that, in cutting themselves off from their father, he and Ann "did a *terrible* thing"; Kate will tell Joe that he must clarify his own guilt with Chris and "make it clear to him that you know you did a *terrible* thing"; and in the opening scene, Chris observed, to Joe, that allowing Kate to continue in her delusion that Larry is alive is "a *terrible* mistake". *Terrible* is a suitable word to describe the tragic knowledge, which, when all the characters reveal what they know, will trigger the eventual tragedy which, even in Act 2, is almost ready to erupt.

George says that their treatment of their father means "we can never be forgiven"; but he and Ann can be, because they acknowledge their mistake and can put it right. When we put this idea - that the children have done something their parents cannot forgive- upside down, we have an accurate vision of the climax of the tragedy, in which it becomes clear that Joe has done something so bad - not just the original deception, but the continual daily deceptions since - that he cannot be forgiven (by Chris), and so must die.

George is wearing his father's hat, because he has come to represent him, and convey his version of events, and his judgment that Ann must not become part of the Keller family by marriage. Steve has asked him to wear the hat, to step into his shoes as the acting head of the family.

There will naturally be tension between Chris, who wants Ann to marry him, and George, who doesn't want this marriage to take place. Chris tells George not to be "the voice of God"- a reference both to George's function in the play as the teller of the real, plain truth, and to a technique in Greek tragedy, which often introduces a god (the so-called "deus ex machina") to resolve the outcome of the plot and direct the audience's emotional responses to issues of morality, guilt and punishment. In attaching this tag to George, Miller is emphasising that the key to the tragedy lies in what George is about to reveal.

And he reveals the key facts immediately; Steve had to ring Joe twice, for instructions, and he only did what Joe had told him to do. Joe's absence ("Sick! He suddenly gets the flu!") was suspicious, because it put space between him and the factory and the decision, and he was able to deny the phone call, because there was no proof of it.

Joe knows very well that the absence of proof does not mean something is untrue, but it does make that thing harder to believe- he tells Chris that Kate will never accept that Larry is dead, because "there's no body and no grave".

Just as Kate had tried, and failed, to use what we might call emotional truth ("Listen to your heart!") to persuade Ann to wait for Larry, so George now appeals to Chris' instinctive emotional knowledge - "You know in your heart Joe did it". Chris will admit a little later that this is so, but, for now, both he and Ann believe (because they want to believe) that the accepted version of events - which will allow them to marry - is the true one.

Chris is not conscious of the irony, when he says that Steve would "throw the blame on somebody else because he's not man enough to take it himself"- he simply has the wrong man here, but it is an accurate assessment of Joe, whom he is trying to defend.

George hints at Joe's preoccupation with materialism, when he defines Ann as "one item he's not going to grab". He says that "everything they have is covered with blood"; a judgment with the moral authority which leads Chris to declare again - less mockingly, this time - that George is "The Voice of God!".

George argues that the fact that Chris is not a formal co-owner of the business means he knows it is tainted. Chris suddenly admits that George is right ("I know the answer") but he wants his mother to be protected from the truth - a truth which she already knows perfectly well, but will not acknowledge in public.

George complies with Chris' wish to avoid a confrontation, and Miller writes a scene with George and Kate (and Lydia) which almost allows Kate to seduce George into the old nostalgia and the sleepy acceptance of the lazy status quo built on the family lies - he says "she makes it seem so nice around here". Kate urges him to abandon his high ideals and be more self-interested (like a true Keller) - "Stop being a philosopher, and look after yourself".

When Joe appears, the tone of the dialogue reverts to that of a shoot-out. George tells Joe that Steve is ill, not with heart trouble, but in his soul. This is the language of the priest/confessor. As Joe makes the offer to give Steve "a place with me"- as though Steve has accepted his own guilt! - George confronts Joe

with the truth, that Steve "hates your guts".
Joe's defence - that Steve has never taken
responsibility for anything – confuses George,
who is "trying to judge him".

The combined charm offensive of Kate and Joe
has worked on George, who wonders at "the
whole atmosphere" and how "at home" he
feels. At the precise moment where he seems
to have given up his mission - to confront Joe
with the fact of Steve's innocence, and Joe's
abominable lies - Kate and Joe disclose the
truth that Joe has never been ill, and that,
therefore, the apparent reason for his absence
from the factory was another lie - a tactical,
cowardly and cold-blooded one.

George works out the implications of this while
Frank – comically - returns with the horoscope.
At first, he "stands perfectly still". He sums up
the truth in one sentence to Ann- "He simply
told your father to kill pilots, and covered
himself in bed!". But Ann will not listen, and she
and Chris force George off stage, into a taxi
and out of the play.

George is only in the play for 20% of the time.
He comes from the outside world, with the truth
- Steve's testimony. The description of him as
"the voice of God" is, therefore, accurate. For

the audience, he serves to establish where the guilt really lies. It is only when the audience appreciates the true scale of Joe's wrongdoing - once we understand to what extent he is himself unreliable in his excuses and justifications - that the play can move on to its climax.

Miller gives us, in George, a son who makes a proper judgment of two fathers - his own and Chris'. By the end of Act 2, he has put Chris in a position where he will have to do the same. The difference George makes is that, without his intervention, bringing Steve's hat and Steve's truth, we would still side with Joe. Joe's self-justifications become pathetic and weak, in the audience's view, in Act 3; in Act 2, George has defined the moral ground on which Joe must be judged by his own son.

Steve Deever

If Joe Keller is the tragic hero, Steve is an anti-hero. He is described, even by his own son, as a liar and a frightened mouse. His wrongful imprisonment has left him without a voice, and soon, George says, all that will be left of him will be a smell. The wrongs done to him have reduced him to nothing.

Joe makes out that Steve was always a "little man", "scared of loud voices", "a fool". He rehearses his well-practised assessment of their father to both Ann and George, separately, in Act 1 and Act 2 - a form of pre-emptive defence in the shape of a ruthless character assassination. If Joe is your friend, who needs enemies?

Miller has deprived Steve of a means of communicating the truth, by making Ann and George condemn him so strongly that they have not even written to him since he was sentenced, let alone visited him, and by making him estranged from his wife; it is only Ann's plan to marry Chris which has finally prompted George to speak to him.

Steve is the underdog. Unable to speak, he finds a way of telling the truth when George agrees to wear his hat, and represent him at the Kellers'. So - as with Larry - even the apparent lack of a way of communicating does not stop him from finally sending the truth to those who should know it, and whose lives will be turned upside down when they have to confront it.

Larry Keller

Larry has been dead for three and a half years, but he keeps appearing, so to speak. He is on stage at the start of the play, in the form of the tree dedicated to his memory, and at the end, where his letter to Ann is the final judgment or sentence on his father's crimes.

The tree is an ambiguous symbol. George goads Chris with it, asking whether it is there to stop them from forgetting Larry. Kate sees its splitting in the storm as a sign that he is still alive, and she sees it as a constricting object too - there is more light without it.

Joe praises Larry as the less complex of his two sons, and the one who was uninterested in social morality- "He understood the way the world is made. He listened to me." This view of Larry turns out to be ironic for Joe, because Larry's judgment of him is simple and moral, when Chris eventually reads his letter aloud - "if I had him here now I could kill him". Larry's suicide makes Joe's suicide inevitable, and right.

Kate (who, according to Sue, thinks she is "psychic") keeps Larry alive simply by refusing to believe that he is dead. As Chris points out, anyone who takes so long to return home from the war must be either reluctant to do so, or unable to.

The other characters often describe Kate's refusal to face the fact that Larry is dead as crazy or insane. She dreams about him, and the horoscope she has asked Frank to research is another attempt to justify her irrational hope.

Kate, though, also uses the myth of Larry to keep order in her world - because, if Joe is responsible for Larry's death, he has committed the unforgivable crime of killing his own son. This double motivation for Kate to keep believing in Larry's survival is one of the cleverest things in the play.

Chris complains that his mother's constant talk of Larry makes their lives sterile and empty - "We're like at a railroad station waiting for a train that never comes in". Miller uses the idea that Larry had been engaged to Ann to force change - Kate can only accept Chris' plan to marry Ann if she accepts that Larry is dead - and to allow the buried truth to be revealed.

Ann is so motivated to marry Chris - in order to escape her own loneliness - that she is willing to confront Kate with the truth that will kill her self-deception; the proof that Larry is dead, and that he killed himself.

What appears to be the tragic death of Larry turns out to trigger a further tragedy- the tragedy of his father's suicide. It is unclear whether Joe's death will enable Chris to marry Ann after all; Kate tells him to "Live", but he has already made plain his abhorrence at the idea of owning a business built on the proceeds of crime.

Larry speaks from an unreachable place - the grave - rather as Steve Deever speaks from his prison cell. Both of them inject a fatal dose of truth into the infection which is the complacent life of the Keller family. It is an odd coincidence that, at almost the same time Miller was writing Larry into his play, JB Priestley was using Eva Smith in "An Inspector Calls" in exactly the same way - as a character whose death exposes the guilt of those who continue to live, but who caused her suicide.

Your Exam

In June 2016, this play will be examined as part of Component 2 or Component 3.

This guide has been written in a way which addresses the assessment objectives; you are expected to have your own ideas about what Miller is saying to us via the medium of the play, and to comment on its language, structure and form. You must show that you are familiar both with the content of the play and with the ideas and attitudes which underpin it; some are contextual, because of the time and the place where Miller was writing (post-War America, in the years up to 1947).

In Component 2, you will have a choice of two questions- one passage-based, the other requiring you to analyse the play more widely. You cannot take your text with you, so you need to be able to refer to relevant quotations from memory. If you choose to write about the passage, you will need to analyse the language in it.

In all essays, you will need to develop a clearly organised point of view, with supporting evidence. Analysing language relates to stagecraft, the way the audience responds to the action, and Miller's use of revelation, dramatic tension and irony.

If this is not your strength, you should choose the other question, which will have more to do with the wider themes, meaning, and characterisation in the play as a whole.

Component 3 allows you to use an unmarked copy of the play, but there is no choice of question.

In both cases, you have 45 minutes to produce your essay, and it makes up 25% of your overall mark.

Ask your teachers to go through the mark schemes and the examiners' reports with you. That will impress on you the importance of making a plan for your essay, and of focusing on the question.

Whenever you give an opinion, you must support it with a relevant reference to the text or a sound explanation of Miller's intentions and methods.

I end this guide with two sample essays; would you have answered them in the same way?

You will see from them that what counts is organising what you want to say (your plan), then working steadily and concisely through it.

Your focus must be on answering the question. This means taking it apart, and highlighting the key word (often, that little word "How"). Your plan will give you an argument and a structure, and enable you to organise your material in a sensible sequence. It will lead you to a concise, clear and convincing conclusion. And it will tell you when to stop, because when you have covered all the points in your plan, there is no need to add anything more. Don't be tempted to think "I'll just write another paragraph or two", because that will lose you structure, marks, and time.

Please, please resist the temptation to start writing your answer straightaway, even if many others in the exam room do precisely that. The exam builds in planning time. Use it to plan.

Finally, keep your focus on what the question requires you to do. Check- constantly- that what you are writing is answering the question you have chosen. If it isn't, leave it out.

I wish you every success in your exam.

Essay 1

"Miller uses "All My Sons" as a means of showing us that the American way of life is wrong." To what extent do you agree with this statement, and why?

Miller's play is a tragedy. We empathise with Joe Keller, even as we condemn his habitual cowardice and his casual lies about the weakness of his former business partner Steve Deever (which he has almost come to believe in, himself). Joe did something so outrageous, in shipping the faulty engine parts, that he forfeits his place in society, and must die to atone for his fatal flaw and his tragic mistake; in doing so, he goes some way towards redeeming himself in the eyes of the audience, and atoning for his crime against society.

The play is about the importance of conscience, personal morality and social responsibility. We all face situations where we choose whether to tell the truth or lie; Miller says that lies will out, whether there are mitigating motives or not. The truth about the edifice of lies on which the Keller family's prosperity is built emerges when the lie about Larry runs out of time, because Chris' intention to marry Ann forces the issue; she produces his suicide note.

Joe's is the largest crime, but Kate is complicit in it too. As Larry's mother, she does not want to face the finality of his death, but the myth that he is still alive also protects Joe; if Larry is dead, Joe killed him, which is something forbidden by God, in Kate's view of the world. Chris and Joe worry (as does Jim, her doctor) that the shock of the truth might harm her health further - she says that, if Larry is dead, she will shoot herself. We cannot be sure that this is an exaggeration.

The Kellers' tragedy is a domestic one; it takes place in their secluded back yard, out of the view of their fellow citizens or the courts. Joe and Kate appear to have achieved the American dream. Joe has a "nice, flexible" plant. He has overcome the disadvantage of minimal education (one year at night school) to build a business which he intends to be his legacy for Chris. After George's awkward observation that Chris is not yet formally involved in the ownership of the business (J O Keller), the end of the play accelerates that change of ownership quite brutally.

Sue Bayliss constantly cajoles Jim to make more money for her; Jim tells Chris and Kate that, in forcing him to give up his dream of medical research in New Orleans, Sue forced him into an unhappy compromise - hence the bitter taste their supposedly affectionate conversations early in the play exhibit. Joe defends his lies and his crimes by reminding Kate that she, too, had wanted money. He seeks to excuse his mistakes, in a way that King Lear, Macbeth, Othello or Oedipus never would. The theme of men refusing to take responsibility for their own choices and actions runs through the play. The fault appears to be Steve's; but it is, in truth, Joe's.

Joe, then, is a tragic hero, but a small one, in a small American suburb. He has no interest in the wider world - he only reads the small ads in the paper- and he praises his missing son, Larry, for his understanding that the building line of their home sets a boundary against the world beyond it, while he criticises Chris for his less narrow view. Chris has returned from the war with a reputation for being "such a killer"; his parents fear him, and they feel they do not understand him and his desire to inspire people to be "better than it's possible to be" (Sue, Act 2). It is his principles they do not understand - the war has given him a sense of responsibility and morality which is quite alien to Joe. Just before Joe shoots himself, Chris is insisting to Kate that "you can be better".

In many families, children come to feel some sort of contempt for their parents. In Chris' case, when his idealised vision of his father is shattered he feels total contempt.

Miller was interested in the dynamics of family life and the conflict between fathers and sons. The domestic setting is important; Joe does not set foot outside his garden and house, and he chooses to end his life at home.

Nonetheless, Joe is the product of small-town America, with its poor education and its poor level of care for others. Judgments are based on appearance, and driven by money; Jim calls on patients who are not ill, and charges them fees; George compliments Joe on his factory, because it looks large and modern; the neighbours have switched from labelling Joe a murderer to playing poker with him; George and Ann have rejected their own father completely, because they have not questioned whether the appeal court decision was right or wrong. Chris finds that the sacrifices in war have had no more impact on the local community than a "bus accident". No-one here cares much about anyone but themselves. The Kellers are mediocre because they reflect the values of a mediocre society.

We can therefore conclude that Chris' idealism is not "phony", as Sue calls it, but real, and a good thing. In calling for the individual to live a more responsible and "better" life, Chris is close to Miller's own view of post-war America. The domestic tragedy therefore has a wider social dimension. Miller said that he wanted to convey, through the play, the sense that "very little had changed" after the War; he was surprised to find that the theatre-going public understood and agreed with him.

920 words

Essay 2

"Joe Keller is responsible for multiple deaths. To what extent do you feel sympathy for him, and why?"

Joe Keller's crimes are very serious, however we choose to explain them. He did not mean to cause the death of pilots, or of his own son, but he did. He seems to have no remorse about being free and blameless in his community, while he has framed Steve, shirked responsibility, and profited from the immoral success retaining his contract with the Army enabled him to achieve.

It is contemptible that he has allowed the truth to be buried, and that he has no conscience until he is final cornered with his guilt. He is scared that George is coming to reopen the case "for the nuisance value" or for revenge; he has no regard for the truth.

Miller manages the plot so that we do not know that Joe is even loosely associated with crime until the latter part of Act 1, and it is only Steve's account to George - which George brings with him in Act 2 - which leads us to challenge the accepted version, and Joe's apparent innocence. Then we wait again for the full force of Joe's "sins" to emerge in the form of Larry's letter right at the end of the play.

Joe defends himself, to Kate, saying that he did what he did not because he was a coward or selfish, but because his family is all that matters ("I got a family……..nothin' is bigger!). When he says, passionately, that "if there is something bigger than that I'll put a bullet in my head!" he goes on to have to do just that. Joe's error is as much a misjudgment as a crime, seen through his own eyes.

The other mitigating factor is Joe's lack of education. "Put out" at the age of ten, he had to make his own way in the world, and has spent forty years building a business he hoped to pass on to Chris. He tried to educate himself at night school for a year, but he remains an ignoramus/stupid/ stolid/ peasant-like; he describes himself as "ignorant", and Kate tells Chris that she and Joe are "Dumb...stupid". He is therefore unable, by his nature and upbringing, to see the need to do the right thing- he is a survivor who has learnt to compensate for his weaknesses and hide them.

Joe "infuriates" Chris with his "talent for ignoring things". We share his frustration, but we can see why Joe's family is such a comfort to him, and so vital to his self-image ("A father is a father"). His desire to hide the truth is not purely cowardice; he thinks it is in his family's interests, and Kate has to correct him, in Act 3 ("it don't excuse it that you did it for the family").

Although he is slow and reluctant to face the consequences of his disastrous choices, Joe finally does so with a quiet dignity that borders on the heroic. He knows when the time to resist is over; he maintains the face of the practised poker player he is, and determines his own fate, before his wife and son can intervene. Larry's voice from beyond the grave makes it impossible, as Chris says, for Joe to "blame the world"; he has to take responsibility, at last.

We would expect to feel alienated from a character who has done what Joe has. Chris is alienated, but the audience is not. Miller manages this by making Joe easy-going, generous, a man who enjoys and facilitates the contentment of others; and by keeping the truth about his guilt hidden, then half-hidden, until the end of the play. The manner of Joe's death is shockingly abrupt, and it cannot atone for the deaths of so many young men, and Larry; but, in recognising and accepting that "they were all my sons", he does what he can to make things better, and to be the better person and father which Chris has insisted he must be.

660 words

Gavin Smithers is a private tutor, covering Broadway, Chipping Campden and the North Cotswolds. He has an English degree from Oxford University, and a passion for helping others to discover the joy and satisfaction of great literature.

And finally ...if there's anything you're not sure about and your teacher can't help, contact the author – grnsmithers@hotmail.co.uk

Gavin's Guides are short books packed with insight. Their key aim is to help you raise your grade!

Understanding J.B. Priestley's An Inspector Calls
Understanding George Orwell's Animal Farm
Understanding William Golding's Lord of the Flies
Understanding Charles Dickens' Great Expectations
Understanding John Steinbeck's Of Mice and Men
Understanding Emily Dickinson's Set Poems
Understanding Edward Thomas' Set Poems
Understanding Harper Lee's To Kill A Mockingbird
Understanding Andrew Marvell's Cromwell & Eulogy Poems

Printed in Great Britain
by Amazon